Developing Sustainable Energy Projects in Emerging Markets

Developing Sustainable Energy Projects in Emerging Markets

Francis Ugboma

BEP

BUSINESS EXPERT PRESS

Leader in applied, concise business books

First published in 2021 by
Business Expert Press, LLC
222 East 46th Street, New York, NY 10017
www.businessexpertpress.com

ISBN-13: 978-1-63742-109-3 (paperback)
ISBN-13: 978-1-63742-110-9 (e-book)

Business Expert Press Economics and Public Policy Collection

Collection ISSN: 2163-761X (print)
Collection ISSN: 2163-7628 (electronic)

First edition: 2021

10 9 8 7 6 5 4 3 2 1

To my late father, for giving me the gift of intellectual curiosity.

Description

An essential primer in the core principles of Sustainable Energy project development this book sets out the common building blocks of sustainable energy projects and provides the practical tools required to develop the stages of a project through concept, design, feasibility, and reality.

It takes a holistic approach to the development and financing of such projects, setting out the technical, commercial, and financial aspects in a straightforward and practical manner. It sets out a first principles-based approach to developing sustainable projects in markets which are not, typically, extensively covered by project finance handbooks and which, in themselves, offer a particular set of challenges to the would-be developer.

While the theory behind each topic will be introduced in order to provide the necessary grounding, the book is very much directed toward the practitioner and students who are considering a career in sustainability.

It is hoped that the reader is left with a strong foundation in a core set of guiding principles that can be applied to a wide range of sustainable energy projects in any geographical location.

Keywords

sustainability; project financing; project development; emerging markets; frontier markets; energy; renewable energy; sustainable energy; climate change; alternative energy; energy transition; developing markets

Contents

Foreword

Francis Ugboma sets out here to assist developers of sustainable energy projects *in successfully framing and ultimately delivering the project ... This can only happen when we have secured the required financing for our projects ... the financial perspective plays as great a part as the technical and commercial considerations.* His mission is an important one, because too few would-be developers understand this at the outset; and life is too short to be reinventing the wheel when mankind is in a hurry to heal the planet.

I learned the disciplines of project development and risk management at Enron in its pre-scandalous heyday when it was transforming the energy world for the better. There, as a Board director of Enron Europe and also of its flagship powerplant Teesside Power (a huge project-financed CHP in England), I saw ample proof of a vital truth. People who understand the financial and risk aspects *before* they embark on their projects and transactions do much better business than those who unexpectedly find themselves confronting the demands for rigor and conformity with the norms of financing that are made by many of the agencies they will meet as they progress their plans.

Even if these demands were to be arbitrary, developers would still need to meet them—because they are being made by the people who hold the purse strings! But they are not arbitrary and should not be resented as some kind of unwarranted hurdle or barrier. On the contrary, they represent sound disciplines, informative metrics, and proven structures, providing a critical, independent sanity-check on the viability of the project. The financiers and consultants are indeed *marking the developer's homework*, as Francis puts it. To know in advance what criteria they bring to bear, and to be positioned to meet them first time, can only be positives for any project.

That's not just for reasons of avoiding wasted time. The book quotes Mark Carney as saying that the global movement toward sustainable energy is *the greatest commercial opportunity of our time*, and very large amounts of money are being mobilized accordingly. But that doesn't mean financiers will drop their standards when it comes to project selection wherever in the world that project is situated. There is a well-known saying (attributed to Emerson): *Build a better mousetrap, and the world will beat a path to your door*: but that can be misleading. Are you so sure your mousetrap really is that much better? If you have been guided by the relevant financial and risk management precepts from the start, you can present a much more confident case, with a better chance of succeeding. Conversely, if you haven't had those principles in mind ab initio, you may not be able to retro-fit them into your project when the bankers start asking questions. You can't fatten the livestock on market day.

More than 20 years ago, after leaving Enron, I was one of small group that founded an energy services company and Francis was one of our earliest and most successful new hires. As we built that company for eventual flotation on the stock market, we took pains to acquaint ourselves with how banks and investors would assess our business model in due course; the norms they would be looking for, the metrics they would apply. These considerations translated into disciplines they would expect us to implement. Following this prescription became second nature to us, and the business we built thrived accordingly, enabling us to go public as we had hoped and planned. They were good disciplines and served us well.

Francis has gone on to gain many other valuable experiences in the energy sector and is imparting much of this wisdom here. He has met, and met successfully, the requirements that financiers will make of developers. The structures and disciplines he describes are "the way of the world" as regards financing sustainable energy projects, and if perhaps that world is less familiar to players in frontier and emerging markets, with this book he is doing them a service indeed.

Nick Perry
March 2021

Preface

Everything around us is a manifestation of energy. To understand this statement, we must recall the laws of thermodynamics. The first law states that matter and energy can neither be created nor destroyed, only transformed. The second law states that in any such transformation the capacity of that energy to do useful work is diminished. The earth is a self-sustaining energy system therefore everything around us is a manifestation of energy.

The appropriation of energy, as it applies to the natural world—that is to say individuals and species—would require that those individuals and species that possess the largest net energy surplus could dedicate more time to their reproduction. By the same logic, those economies that possess the largest net surplus of energy would therefore be in a better position to thrive.

This is the reason why I chose to write this book on renewable or sustainable energy. The economy is a system of energy use and those economies that this book is focused on, those least developed economies and emerging economies have traditionally been those that are typified by lower GDP than that of the developed world.

It would therefore be beneficial to those economies that are struggling for them to increase their capacity for energy usage, however, they are faced with a world where climate change has been largely acknowledged and that an energy transition toward low-carbon technologies is a requirement for human survival. This transition is well under way in much of the developed world, but we need to assure a transition to low-carbon energy systems in the developing world.

This book is directed at developers of renewable energy projects in countries where access to finance, technologies, expertise, and regulatory frameworks is a challenge. So, as the reader of this book there are three questions to ask yourself:

1. What is the level of energy investment required for your energy infrastructure project?

2. What is the total energy appropriation of the economy in which your project is located?

3. How much energy is used to produce one unit of GDP in that economy?

The answers to those three questions will fundamentally affect how the project should be developed and framed in the future. My intention is for this book to assist you in successfully framing and ultimately delivering the project.

Acknowledgments

Firstly, I would like to express my gratitude to the publishers for offering me the platform to share my ideas with a wide audience. I would also like to thank my research assistant Desislava Todorova who, along with research, proofreading, and editorial support, did particularly helpful work on case studies and SROI.

Special thanks to Dmitrijs Artusins who kindly agreed to be interviewed and for whose invaluable experience on project development I am grateful to be able to share with you in these pages. Big thanks go also to Nick Perry, who over the course of our two-decade-long relationship has acted as colleague, mentor, referee, and friend.

Finally, I would like to thank my better half Helen, who proofread, chopped, changed, and was the driving factor in getting the manuscript into shape. She is my rock whose patience, love, and support cannot have a value placed on it.

CHAPTER 1

Introduction and Notes to the Reader

From my over twenty years of experience as a project developer, the process of financing an energy project can be compared to sailing a boat over the high seas. As a sailor possesses a collection of essential implements—a seagoing vessel, detailed plans, a map, navigational equipment, and food supplies—so too does a project developer require their own specific tools.

Taking an energy project to financial close (the point at which all financings has been secured and that the construction phase is ready to begin) and beyond operation requires the timely execution of a series of steps. These steps include feasibility studies, Front End Engineering and Design (FEED) studies, ESIAs, Engineering, Procurement and Construction (EPC) contracts, Power Purchase Agreements (PPAs), financing agreements, and Operations and Maintenance (O&M) contracts, among many others.

A breakdown of the main elements that underpin project finance are summarized in Table 1.1.

Even if you make sound progress putting the above elements in place, the completion of the project is far from guaranteed. Any one of the abovementioned agreements may "fail" at any point. Other factors beyond the control of the developer can cause major delays or even cause developers to shelve plans completely after having invested time, effort, and substantial amounts of money.

This book aims to assist burgeoning developers by showing them how to reduce the risk of external factors undermining a project; it seeks to help the reader to ensure that all of those elements that are under the developer's control are put together in the best possible manner given the resources at the developer's disposal. Good project developers are drawn to the challenge. This book is for the intrepid sailor, the project developer,

Table 1.1 Breakdown of project finance elements

	Name	Description
1.	Feasibility studies	Your project concept will have to be studied and deemed practicable by a credible third party.
2.	Environmental and social impact assessment	The project's potential impacts will have to be assessed and measured by independent assessors.
3.	Detailed engineering and design	From feasibility, an engineering consultant will develop the design and technical configuration of the project.
4.	Offtake/Sales agreements	The output of your project, energy supply, will need to be purchased on a long-term basis by a creditworthy buyer or Off-taker. In some cases, this Off-taker could be a government entity such as a national utility company.
5.	Guarantees	Legal contracts that support the creditworthiness of the offtake agreements in cases where the buyer is not deemed as sufficiently creditworthy by the project's lenders.

who is focused on renewable energy in frontier and emerging (developing) market, who dares to sail to parts that are uncharted and yet present enormous potential.

The book draws on my experience of developing energy projects under challenging circumstances in every corner of the globe. Such projects include onshore and offshore wind farms, solar photovoltaic (PV) farms, biomass, and waste-to-energy plants.

We shall take a holistic approach to the development and financing of such projects by laying out the common building blocks of sustainable energy projects. This will provide the reader with the practical tools required to work their way through concept, design, feasibility, and reality. In the interests of clarity, the words entrepreneur, project developer and student are interchangeable.

While this book is written with very much the developer at its center, it can be of use to others as well. For example, policymakers, investors, bankers, lawyers, contractors, government agencies, and nongovernmental agencies can all draw some benefit from the book. The fact that these are usually key stakeholders in such projects is no coincidence and their role as actors in the energy sector will be examined in more detail later.

Having a firm grasp on the essentials of the framework will increase one's chances of success; however, it offers no guarantee. My intention is to put the reader on the path toward mastering the core tools and frameworks for developing a sustainable energy project to the point where the project's location (developing or otherwise) matters less.

> "The objective for the private finance work for COP26 is simple; to make sure that every private finance decision takes climate change into account."
>
> —Mark Carney, UN Special Envoy on climate action,
> February 2020

CHAPTER 2

What Is Sustainable Energy and Project Finance?

What Does Sustainability Mean?

The dictionary definition of the term "sustainable" means "able to be maintained at a certain rate or level." We increasingly see the use of this as a prefix for many disciplines and sectors—architecture, clothing, tourism, development, and so on. In terms of this book, sustainable energy projects are those that account for three aspects of a project's impacts: economic, social, and environmental. Given that we are on a path to an energy transition, renewable energy projects are, or should be, sustainable. The principles presented in this book and the types of projects that are covered utilize the technologies listed below:

- Wind (Onshore and offshore)
- Solar (large scale and small scale)
- Biofuels
- Biomass and waste

In 2015, the United Nations (UN) adopted a prominent leadership role on sustainability by defining a comprehensive set of goals, 17 of them, around the concept of sustainability. These goals, which are listed below and covered in more detail in the chapter on measuring sustainability, will increasingly feature in our daily lives as the world, in particular the energy sector, transitions from fossil fuels into a low-carbon future:

- Goal 1. End poverty in all its forms everywhere.
- Goal 2. End hunger, achieve food security and improved nutrition and promote sustainable agriculture.

- Goal 3. Ensure healthy lives and promote well-being for all at all ages.
- Goal 4. Ensure inclusive and equitable quality education and promote lifelong learning opportunities for all.
- Goal 5. Achieve gender equality and empower all women and girls.
- Goal 6. Ensure availability and sustainable management of water and sanitation for all.
- Goal 7. *Ensure access to affordable, reliable, sustainable, and modern energy for all.*
- Goal 8. Promote sustained, inclusive, and sustainable economic growth, full and productive employment, and decent work for all.
- Goal 9. Build resilient infrastructure, promote inclusive and sustainable industrialization, and foster innovation.
- Goal 10. Reduce inequality within and among countries.
- Goal 11. Make cities and human settlements inclusive, safe, resilient, and sustainable.
- Goal 12. *Ensure sustainable consumption and production patterns.*
- Goal 13. *Take urgent action to combat climate change and its impacts.*
- Goal 14. Conserve and sustainably use the oceans, seas, and marine resources for sustainable development.
- Goal 15. Protect, restore, and promote sustainable use of terrestrial ecosystems, sustainably manage forests, combat desertification, and halt and reverse land degradation and halt biodiversity loss.
- Goal 16. Promote peaceful and inclusive societies for sustainable development, provide access to justice for all and build effective, accountable, and inclusive institutions at all levels.
- Goal 17. Strengthen the means of implementation and revitalize the global partnership for sustainable development.

Within Goal 7, which looks at the subject of energy provision, are a specific set of objectives that are particularly relevant to the contents of this book:

1. *By 2030 ensure universal access to affordable, reliable, and modern energy services.*
2. *By 2030, increase substantially the share of renewable energy in the global energy mix.*
3. *By 2030, enhance international cooperation to facilitate access to [renewable] energy and promote investment in energy infrastructure and clean energy technology.*
4. *By 2030, expand infrastructure and upgrade technology for supplying modern and sustainable for all in developing countries.*

Everything you read in this book can help you as a developer achieve the objectives laid out within these SDGs. Renewable energy projects are sustainable projects and their successful development requires an approach that is holistic, which takes into account all impacts that energy projects provoke.

What this means in practice is that all the benefits and costs, in other words both positive and negatives impacts, should be considered when developing the sustainable energy projects of the future.

What Are Emerging and Frontier Markets?

The most well-known emerging markets are Brazil, China, and India, known collectively as the "BRICS." Farida Khambata of the International Finance Corporation (IFC) coined the term "frontier" markets back in 1992. These markets are less advanced than emerging markets but more established than Least Developed Countries (LDCs). They are known as frontier because, while still being "investable," they are less liquid, smaller, and therefore riskier than emerging markets. Such markets present a challenge for attracting any inward investment, even for so-called stable infrastructure projects.

The UN, many financial institutions, and the major market indexes such as Standard and Poor's (S&P), Financial Times Stock Exchange

Group (FTSE), and Morgan Stanley Capital International (MSCI) all publish lists on the different classes of countries. Table 2.1 attempts to categorize a selection of countries as accurately as possible, but the reader is advised that a country's classification can frequently change depending on the source of information.

Countries in developed, emerging, frontier and LDC markets are summarized in Table 2.1.

Table 2.1 *Countries in developed, emerging, frontier, and LDC markets*

Developed countries or G7	Emerging Markets	Frontier Markets	LDCs
Canada, France, Germany, Italy, Japan, United Kingdom, United States	Brazil, China, Colombia, Greece, Hong Kong, Israel, India, Indonesia, Malaysia, Mexico, Philippines, Poland, Russia, Singapore, South Africa, South Korea, Saudi Arabia, Taiwan, Thailand, Turkey, United Arab Emirates	Argentina, Bahrain, Bosnia & Herzegovina, Botswana, Bulgaria, Côte d'Ivoire, Croatia, Cyprus, Ecuador, Estonia, Egypt, Gabon, Ghana, Jamaica, Jordan, Kazakhstan, Kenya, Kuwait, Latvia, Lebanon, Lithuania, Macedonia, Mali,. Malta, Mauritius, Morocco, Namibia, Nigeria, Oman, Pakistan, Panama, Papua New Guinea, Qatar, Romania, Senegal, Serbia, Slovakia, Slovenia, Sri Lanka, Trinidad & Tobago, Tunisia, Ukraine, Vietnam, Zambia	Afghanistan, Angola, Bangladesh, Benin, Bhutan Burkina Faso, Burundi, Cambodia, Central African Republic, Chad, Comoros, Democratic Republic of Congo, Djibouti, Eritrea, Gambia, Guinea, Guinea-Bissau, Haiti, Lao People's Demo-cratic Republic, Lesotho, Liberia, Madagascar, Myanmar, Nepal, Niger, Sierra Leone, Solomon Islands, Timor-Leste, Tuvalu, Vanuatu, Tanzania, Togo, Uganda, Yemen

When researching the energy profile of developing countries, one notices a pattern between growth in GDP and growth in energy consumption. Studies show that in developed countries energy consumption per capita is up to five times that in lesser-developed countries. To have developing countries catch up to this rate of consumption will not be sustainable.

There is a strong argument to say that developing countries can show the way in doing more with less. Increase the portion of renewables in the energy mix by developing more renewable energy projects while simultaneously using energy more efficiently.

What Is Project Finance?

There is no single acknowledged definition for project finance. In its essence, project finance means that lenders make loans for the purposes of the development of a project. For the purposes of this book, project finance means the use of a specially created Project Company, which owns all of the cash flows and risks (assets and liabilities) specific to a project. Project finance usually involves high leverage (debt-to-equity ratio) and a future set of cash flows that fund the returns required by the debt and equity providers to the project.

There is usually only a single asset on the Project Company's balance sheet (e.g., a wind farm or a biomass power plant), which is what distinguishes project finance from corporate finance. In corporate finance, a series of assets on a corporation's balance sheet could come into play, for example to be used as collateral to secure a debt. Project finance therefore involves nonrecourse lending because there are no other assets on the Project Company's balance sheet. Benjamin C. Esty,[1] in *Modern Project Finance*, assigns three distinct features to project companies:

1. Legally independent entities with a very concentrated equity ownership
2. High leverage (>70 percent debt-to-total capitalization)
3. Project companies are founded on a series of legal contracts (40 or more)

---

[1] Esty, B.C. 2004. *Modern Project Finance: A Casebook*, pp. 24–25. Boston: Wiley.

Given the aforementioned, it should be of little surprise that project finance can come with very high transaction and development costs. Ten percent or more of the project's overall costs can be spent well before the project's Financial Close, or final investment decision (FID) is taken. Given the high transaction costs that are involved, project finance is not usually the best option for any project costing less than $80 to $100 million (debt plus equity).

Project financing is particularly important for energy projects in developing markets where at times there exists a high degree of political or country risk that requires mitigation. In these cases, multiple contractual arrangements are made between the host country's government or its agencies and Development Finance Institutions (DFIs) or multilateral lending agencies.

The Importance of Sustainable Energy

The twin crises of the 2008 Global Financial Crisis and the 2020 coronavirus pandemic will lead to a fundamental transformation of economic activity across the globe. For developing countries, this will mean the increasing importance of sustainable energy projects.

In the past, projects in the energy sector have not always been developed with the goal of sustainability in mind. Indeed, history can point to countless examples of where the unforeseen negative costs of a project, known by economists as externalities, are borne by the wider society in an unjust manner.

By keeping a lens of sustainability on your project, you are better placed to avoid potential negative outcomes. Indeed, in this day and age, every aspect of human activity should aspire to be sustainable; this is because the effects of climate change can no longer be ignored. From Greta Thunberg to Pope Francis, the debate on climate action has taken a firm hold in the mainstream.

What all of this means for the reader of this book is encouraging; for us as sustainable energy developers, our main concern is for our projects to become realized. This can only happen when we have secured the required financing for our projects. Financing and sustainability will increasingly become intertwined. As part of the United Kingdom's presidency of the UN's 26th Climate Change Conference in November 2021 (COP26), private finance will be directed toward driving the global economy's transition to a low-carbon future. The overarching goal is for every financial decision to consider climate change.

In practice, this would mean financial institutions embedding a zero-carbon agenda covering all aspects of their activities: risk management, investment decisions, and DFI investing. According to the Bank of England,[2] the wider implications of this can be summarized as follows:

1. Banks, insurers, and investors will demand climate action transparency from companies.
2. Climate Action100+, a group of investors that control over $35 trillion of assets are asking companies for strengthened governance of climate change risks and opportunities to reduce greenhouse gas emissions across the value chain to levels consistent with the Paris Agreement.
3. The Net Zero Asset Owner Alliance, whose members commit to transitioning their investment portfolios to net-zero greenhouse gas emissions by the year 2050, now represents $5 trillion in assets under management.

The UN Special Envoy on climate action, Mark Carney—who himself was formerly Governor of the Bank of England—in his announcement on private finance and climate action noted that "every company, bank, insurer and investor would have to adjust their business models." Furthermore, in doing so we could turn an "existential risk into the greatest commercial opportunity of our time."[3]

With respect to sustainable energy projects in developing countries, rich nations pledged at the 2015 Paris Agreement to mobilize $100 billion per year by 2020 to help developing countries reduce emissions and mitigate climate change. Therefore, the stage should be improving for

---

[2] https://bankofengland.co.uk/news/2020/february/cop26-private-finance-agenda-launched
[3] https://climatechangenews.com/2020/02/27/net-zero-goal-greatest-commercial-opportunity-time-says-mark-carney/

sustainable energy developers focused on developing countries to gain more assistance in financing the types of projects that have traditionally been difficult to finance.

Next Steps

In the next section of this book, we shall go into the core principles of developing and financing sustainable energy projects. This core set can be applicable to different project types and geographic locations. Indeed, these principles can also be applied in a nonproject financing scenario, as the reader will soon learn. We shall look into who are the main actors of a project, their roles and how risk is apportioned across these.

Then we shall explore frontier and emerging markets in more detail. We shall consider what makes these markets more challenging, how they are different from more advanced economies, and how we can apply the core principles in these markets. We shall look at this within the context of renewable energy. Finally, we will examine a case study from real life.

We then look at raising money and attracting the right type of equity investor and lenders to your project. We explore the main elements of term sheets, the various risks, and implications of these. We also look into strategies for negotiation and the concept and practice of due diligence.

Finally, we will look at the concept of sustainable return on investment (SROI) and outline how this can be measured. In doing so, we will examine in more detail the UN's Sustainable Development Goals and build up a framework and methodology for measuring and reporting the SROI.

CHAPTER 3

The Core Principles for Developing and Financing Sustainable Energy Projects: Part I—the Structure of a Project

Project finance involves the raising of debt in order to realize a project that repays this debt through future cash flows. Prior to any such realization, during its development phase, the project will be evaluated in detail for the lenders to be confident in the project's ability to repay the debt.

According to Yescombe,[1] projects involved in project finance possess the following characteristics:

1. The project usually relates to major infrastructure with a long construction period and long operating life.
2. As a result, the financing must also be for a long term (typically 15–25 years).
3. As the lenders rely on the project's future cash flows to repay the debt, interest and fees, the project must be "ring-fenced" (legally and economically self-contained).
4. The project will be carried through a special-purpose legal entity (usually a limited company) whose only business is the project (the "Project Company").

---

[1] Yescombe. E.R. 2014. *Principles of Project Finance*. pp. 7–8, Oxford: Academic Press.

5. High leverage or gearing for example, the project finance debt may cover 79–90 percent of the capital cost of a project.

6. High leverage reduces the blended cost of debt and equity, and hence the overall financing cost of the project.

7. The main security for the lenders are project company's contracts, licenses, or other rights, which are the source of its cash flow.

8. The project has a finite life in which to repay the debt, based on such factors as the length of contracts or licenses, or reserves of natural resources.

9. Nonrecourse finance—the investors in the project company provide no guarantees for the project finance debt.

In such a structure, the financial perspective plays as great a part as the technical and commercial considerations. Developers therefore need to have a strong grasp of finance and by extension the core principles of project finance in order to be best placed to deliver a successful project.

Given its nature, there is an enormous amount of detail required when trying to master project finance. In this book, we are not able to cover the entirety of the detail; rather, this section will highlight the main principles that will be most useful for you as a developer, based on my own experience. We shall define each principle and go through the relevant details needed in order to arm the reader with the requisite understanding to be able to handle the challenges of project development in a practical scenario.

The principles that we shall cover fall into three broad categories:

A. Structure of a project: consisting of issues relating to the project company, the project participants, and the project lifecycle.

B. Financial aspects of a project: such as the project finance markets; raising project finance; and valuation of a project and the financial model.

C. Risk management and legal aspects of a project: encompassing the project agreements and their required content as well as consideration of the main risks and risk allocation.

In this chapter, let us consider the structural aspects of a project.

The Project Company

The developer will set up a specifically created project company whose activities will be focused on all aspects—project development, engineering, studies, fund-raising—of delivering the project. Most project companies I have come across will be set up in tax-favorable jurisdictions and have a wholly owned subsidiary formed in the host country.

When assessing a project, lenders will apply certain criteria toward evaluating the developer, including that of assessing the management team. Developers are usually made up of a blend of "in-house" staff and external consultants with the purpose of covering all of the skills and experience required. We can think of the developer's team having three profiles as the project goes through the development, construction, and finally operations phases. At any rate, the lenders will need to be satisfied that the staff possess the appropriate level of skills and experience.

At the formation of the project company where there is more than one sponsor, a shareholders agreement will be needed to provide for share ownership, voting rights, board representation, appointment of managers, budgeting, disputes, conflicts of interest, dividends, and sales of shares.

An example of the structure for a project company developing a utility-scale solar farm is shown in Figure 3.1.

The project company is set up by the sponsor with equity, which will be used to fund the construction phase alongside the debt provided by the lenders. The mix of debt versus equity will reflect the high leverage that is typical of project finance structures. It should however be carefully noted that in the lead up to this, there will have been project development activities such as the Environmental and Social Impact Assessment (ESIA) and other studies which will have been funded by the sponsors/developer.

The lenders will have agreed to lend into the project company at the point of financial close. Up to financial close, the sponsors/developer are responsible for funding all of the activities of the project company with their own funds. A slight adjustment of the following diagram to illustrate the relationship between the sponsors, developer and project company up to the point of financial close is shown in Figure 3.2.

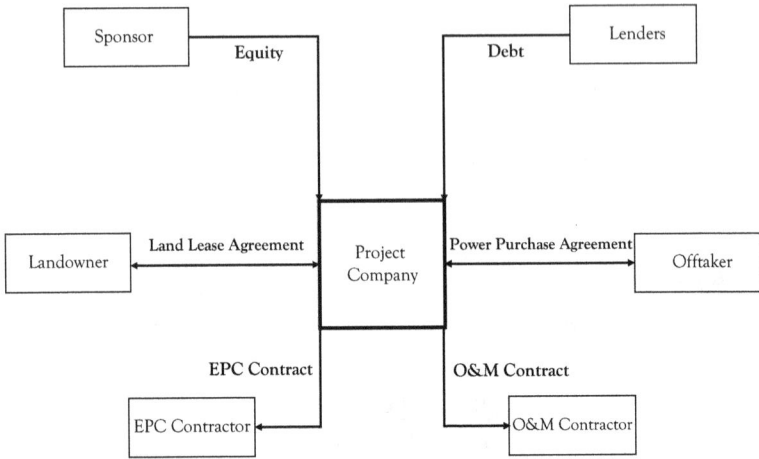

Figure 3.1 Solar farm project structure

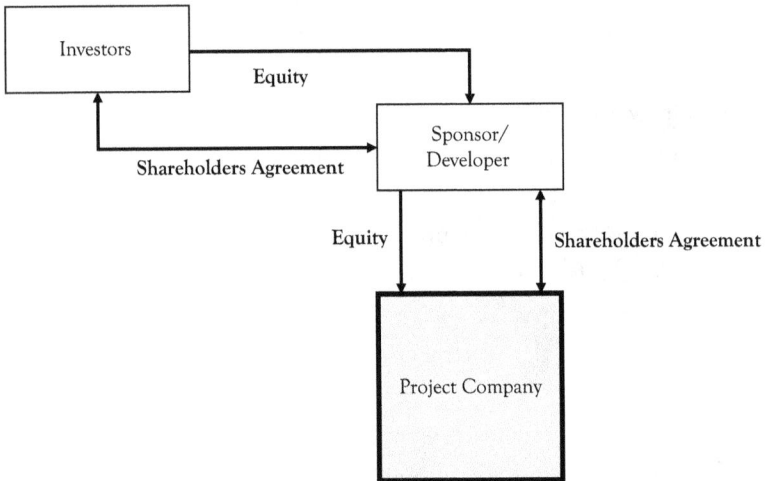

Figure 3.2 Investor/Sponsor/Project company structure

In the case of large-scale solar farms, a developer will usually not purchase the site outright but will enter into a land use/lease agreement with the owner of the land. This agreement will confer rights to the developer to access, develop, and operate on the site in return for lease payments or in some cases revenue sharing. The agreement may require the developer, after the period of the lease is completed, to return the site to its original state thereby incurring decommissioning and other costs.

The equity that the sponsor contributes to the project company could be cash but will also, most likely, be made up of the agreements (e.g., the land lease agreement) and the studies that the developer has carried out as part of the project's development.

The Project Participants

Aside from the developer, there is a host of other actors needed to complete a project. Specialist project developers tend to be lean organizations and hence the services provided by external advisors will be valuable.

The other main participants of the project are as follows:

Host Government or Contracting Authority: Offtaker. In many cases, the host country government also owns the offtaker, for example, in the case of a state-owned utility.

Legal Advisors: Given the nature of interconnected commercial agreements the legal advice provided is vital and will make up a substantial part of the development costs incurred.

Financial Advisors: Financial advice will revolve around the validation of the financial model, navigation of the due diligence process, and the raising and possible syndication of debt from commercial lenders. As this can be a wide-ranging role, depending on the internal capacity of the developer, the scope of activities will determine the cost of the engagement.

Consultants: Engineering consultancies are usually the go to place for developers to carry out up front feasibility studies, ESIAs, pre-Front End Engineering and Design (FEED) and FEED studies. These activities will increase in costs as one progresses through the project lifecycle. The accuracies presented in the calculations are intended to increase certainty around the technical aspects of the project.

Engineering, Procurement and Construction (EPC) Contractor: The EPC contractor will be tasked with constructing and commissioning the project according to the specifications laid out in the FEED documentation. Like any construction project, extensions in time and or materials will have an adverse impact on the cost of the project. Turnkey or lump sum contracts are therefore employed by developers to mitigate their exposure to cost overruns. Only EPC contractors with strong reputations and balance sheets should be considered.

Lenders: Commercial lenders that lend into emerging markets are numerous. We can see a selection of such organizations, which between 2005 and 2015 cumulatively, have assisted projects by over $500 million (Table 3.1).

Investors: The providers of equity investment to the project company and or the developer who do not take an active role in the management of either. These will likely be present at the outset of the project but may come in at the last minute at financial close.

The Project Lifecycle

The lifecycle of a project typically contains three phases, although in the case of offshore wind projects a fourth, decommissioning, will have to be considered.

1. Development
2. Construction
3. Operations
4. Decommissioning (not in the scope of this book)

Table 3.1 Commercial lenders into emerging markets[2]

Name	Assistance ($ millions)
Agence Française de Développement	2,533
China Development Bank	1,000
Nederlandse Financierings-Maatschappij voor Ontwikkelingslanden N.V. (FMO)	521
Asian Development Bank (ADB)	4,227
African Development Bank	1,824
Norfund	883
International Finance Corporation (IFC)	2,394
Inter-American Development Bank (IDB)	3,959
World Bank	8,801

[2] 2017 UNEP Report—Renewable energy and efficiency in developing countries.

Development

The first phase, Development and Project Management, covers all activities related to your project up to financial close. Included in this are activities that secure offtake agreements, planning consents, permissions, and any engineering design work.

For example, a solar farm will require a site on which the resource assessment will have to be performed. A developer can acquire a site in a number of ways, such as through a lease agreement with the owner of the site. In some cases, it may be feasible for the site owner to be an equity partner in the project special purpose vehicle (SPV).

A resource assessment will give an estimate of how much energy can be generated from the site through the life of the project. This can be performed through a combination of desktop analysis and physical site surveys. Projects such as wind and solar may require the deployment of resource measuring equipment at the site for a certain period.

It is advisable at this stage to begin scoping and establishing the terms of reference for an ESIA. This serves the purpose of identifying the potential environmental and social impacts of your project. Local communities, activist groups, and government agencies will need to be consulted on a regular basis.

Many emerging and frontier jurisdictions may not have any statutory provisions covering your project's development. This highlights one of the challenges we face in developing projects in emerging markets. In more developed economies, there is usually a clear idea of the statutory and nonstatutory stakeholders that will need to be consulted. The challenge in this case is for the developer to interact with and possibly educate the relevant government authority about the project in order to determine who needs to be, and who should be, consulted.

It should be clear that to carry out the above will require time and effort and money to be spent. Most developers will not have the in-house expertise to carry out an ESIA or resource assessment. As set out in the previous section, the developer will have to engage external consultants or team up with them as potential equity partners and share the development risk.

Once these initial reports and studies are performed, the developer will engage with an engineering consultancy that will carry out the initial detailed technical studies known as the pre-FEED. This will develop the concept of the energy system to be employed and will provide the basis for the EPC work. A pre-FEED is the precursor to the more detailed FEED, which is carried out to provide the necessary technical and design specifications borne from the studies and assessments carried out earlier in the project. The FEED is a fundamental document that underpins any project finance arrangement. It provides the developer (and investors) with a measure of certainty over costs and will be a determining factor on the operational and financial viability of the project.

The aforementioned summarizes the work involved in the development and project management phase. Clearly, a significant amount of money will need to be spent early on with no guarantees that the project is viable or that the project will be approved. This development risk can be seen as binary given that throughout this phase the project undergoes a series of "go/no go" decision points. From experience, estimates of the costs of this initial work can be up to 10 percent or more of the overall cost of the project.

Construction

Most people would assume that during the phase of construction, installation and commissioning the developer usually takes a back seat. This would be a mistake; while the completion of final investment decision (FID) and financial close is an enormous achievement, the developer needs to maintain strong control over every aspect of the construction and commissioning phase.

Lacking the expertise required to closely supervise the work of the contractor, the developer will appoint an owner's engineer (also known as employer's agent or client engineer). In essence, the role is to protect the developer's interests; in practice this means that while the owner's engineer will be the one overseeing the day-to-day work of the contractor on behalf of the developer, the developer is ultimately responsible.

The developer will need to sign off on the quality of both the materials employed and the works carried out by the contractor. The owner's engineer will ensure that the construction follows the design specification set out in the FEED and meets statutory or prea-greed quality standards. This is to ensure that upon commission-ing the developer takes delivery of an energy system that performs as predicted by the projections of the financial model.

Operations

This is the phase during which the project generates cash flows to repay the lenders and generate a return for the investors. Revenues from sales of energy will be offset by expenditure on items such as operating expenses, debt repayment, maintenance, and servicing. In Figure 3.3, the relative costs at various stages of project development are shown.

Figure 3.3 shows the main cost items and an estimate on their amount for a generic renewable energy project costing $100 million in total. For illustration purposes, we assume a debt equity ratio of 85:15. Taking the aforementioned, the developer will have incurred up to $5 million in devel-opment costs prior to reaching financial close. Furthermore, the developer will have had to raise another $5 million in equity funding on top of the $85 million debt financing.

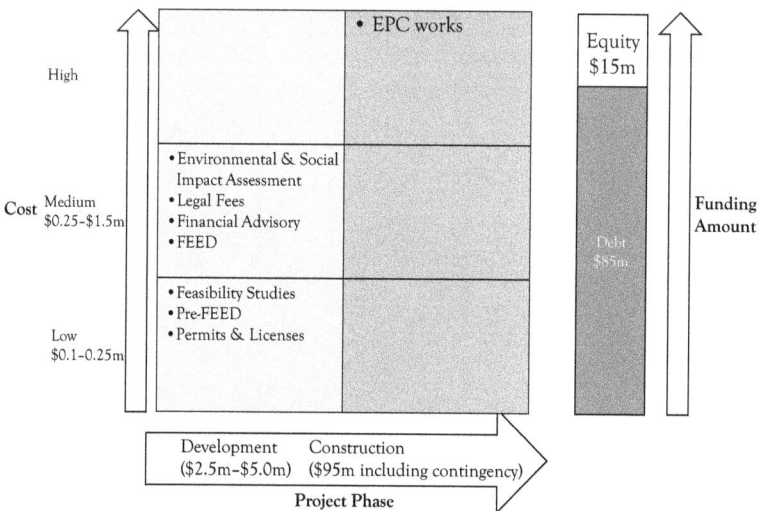

Figure 3.3 Project cost items in development and construction phases

CHAPTER 4

The Core Principles for Developing and Financing Sustainable Energy Projects: Part II—Financial Aspects

Having considered structural principles in the previous chapter, we can now move on to financial matters.

The Project Finance Markets

Typically, the market for raising project finance for a project is the country in which that project is located. While some developing countries are still struggling with the raising of funding in home markets, there are many sources of such funding from providers such as Development Finance Institutions (DFIs) and Export Credit Agencies (ECAs).

However, international organizations such as these lend to projects in U.S. dollars, which brings the risk of foreign exchange fluctuations into the picture. It is, therefore, in many respects, optimal to raise funds locally from organizations who are willing to lend to your project in the local currency and who understand the local conditions in which your project is operating. Some developing countries possess some depth in project finance (e.g., India, Nigeria, and Brazil), meaning that they can lend to projects in the local currency through both commercial and public sector development banks.

Other than loans from commercial and development banks developers can access:

i. Mezzanine debt—subordinated debt from nonbank investors
ii. Vendor finance—can be obtained from equipment manufacturers and repaid once the project begins generating revenues

iii. Islamic finance—applicable to Islamic countries and which adheres to the Koranic prohibition on charging interest

Raising Project Finance

While bonds are used in developed markets, their use is not prevalent in developing countries and hence are not within the scope of this book.

Most commercial banks, regardless of country of operation, will not look at projects with a ticket size of less than $100million. Given the amount of time and effort required to carry out the due diligence to reach Financial Close this makes sense. Once the developer is convinced that the project is feasible, then it makes sense to begin discussions with a commercial bank's project finance team. Early-stage talks will revolve around project particulars and both parties will gain a sense of whether they wish to work together.

The developer may engage with several banks in an effort to gain the best lending conditions but ultimately one single bank will usually be appointed as the "lead arranger" for the project. The lead arranger will underwrite the debt for the project and may bring in other banks as part of a syndicate of lenders. In some cases, the lead arranger is also appointed as the financial advisor.

Once the bank's interest in the project is confirmed, then a Letter of Intent (LOI) or term sheet is issued. This will lay out the headline terms under which the bank will lend to the project and will detail estimates on arrangement fees, interest rates, and conditions. Developers will use this document to gain credibility with other project participants, especially equity investors whose confidence should be boosted by a credible lender's interest in the project.

Term sheets and LOIs are not, however, legally binding documents and developers will be expected to meet certain conditions prior to the achievement of Financial Close. That is to say, even with the signature of the financing documentation and the project agreements, the developer (or more likely Project Company) may still be required to fulfill other conditions precedent before funds can be drawn down to begin construction. It is at the point when funds can be drawn down that the project is said to have achieved Financial Close.

For the due diligence process, the lead arranger will deploy its own experts—legal, financial, technical, and tax—to determine the project's viability. These experts, in effect, are marking the developer's homework and the developer, usually at Financial Close, will pay for their costs.

In addition to commercial banks, there are three other main sources of loans for projects in developing countries:

    i. Export credit agencies
   ii. Bilateral DFIs
  iii. Multilateral DFIs

> *Export Credit Agencies* (ECAs): These provide loans and political and financial risk cover for projects that export capital equipment from their home country. An example of this would be the China Exim-bank providing financing for the sale of solar PV equipment manufactured in China and sold to a project in a developing country. These can be private sector or public sector institutions, but they are usually backed by government support.

> An important characteristic of ECAs is that their support is governed, by consensus, under the Organisation for Economic Co-operation and Development (OECD) Consensus. While not legally binding, this consensus aims to provide a framework under which all ECAs can operate across the globe.

> It should also be noted that some ECAs will not provide full coverage of whatever risk they are insuring and that premiums for their support can be high. It can be that some private sector lenders are not willing to support a project without ECA involvement. As you will note from the below on bilateral DFIs, many ECAs work in concert with bilateral DFIs from their respective countries.

> *Bilateral DFIs*: These are termed "bilateral" because there is one funding government that owns or supports the DFI and the host country in which the project is located. Examples of bilateral DFIs and their respective countries are as follows: Proparco, France; DEG, Germany; and FMO, the Netherlands. Given their bilateral nature, they often work closely in partnership with their own ECAs to finance a project.

Multilateral DFIs: The most notable of these is the World Bank, which, with its affiliates, the International Finance Corporation (IFC), the Multilateral Investment Guarantee Agency (MIGA) and the International Development Association (IDA), work extensively in both developed and developing markets. The IFC's wide portfolio of services, including its ability to lend in local currency to projects in developing countries has been a driver in the growth of project finance markets in these countries. The IDA provides support for the world's poorest countries and MIGA provides political risk guarantees to project companies and their investors.

Other major multilateral DFIs or development banks include the African Development Bank, the Asian Development Bank, the European Bank for Reconstruction, and the European Investment Bank. Smaller multilateral DFIs include the Corporacion Andina de Fomenta (CAF), the Central American Bank for Economic Integration (CABEI), and the Eurasian Development Bank.

When it comes to sourcing funding from multilateral DFIs, one key consideration to take into account is that of "additionality," which means that they often act as a "lender of last resort," when developers cannot find financing from other sources. More relevant to the aims of this book in promoting the development of renewable energy projects is that multilateral DFIs will look to finance projects that correspond closely with the UN's Sustainable Development Goals (SDGs).

Valuation and the Financial Model

The financial model will determine the project's valuation and its viability. Different participants will have a different perspective of what that value is: for instance, lenders will value the project based on the project's ability to repay the debt principal, its interest, and any other fees payable to the lenders.

Equity investors, whose equity investment makes up a small fraction of the total capital deployed will have a different return profile, thanks to the leverage inherent in project finance situations. The developer, when starting out on a project for the first time may want to see some kind of multiple of, say five times, the capital it has spent leading up to Financial Close.

Each of the aforementioned will therefore have their own version of the financial model to manipulate through the course of the project's lifecycle up to Financial Close. At Financial Close, the model is set in stone, usually to reflect the most important participant's (the lenders') perspective.

That being the case, the developer should be the originator of the financial model and have a strong grasp of the inputs, assumptions, and outputs and how these change over the course of the project. Setting up a financial model early in the project's development will serve many benefits:

i. Evaluation of potential returns for the developer and equity investors
ii. Structuring of different financing arrangements and offers of financing from lenders
iii. Attracting the right type of equity investor and comparing equity investment offers

Further down the line, the model can be used to simulate the financial impacts of commercial aspects of the project agreements and as a means of narrowing down key issues as the foundation agreements near signature. In the run up to Financial Close, the model will form a key tool in the lenders' due diligence process and does risk outgrowing the capabilities of its originator, the developer.

Once Financial Close is achieved and the project is operational, the financial model can serve as a budgeting tool for the Project Company that calculates exposures caused by different events. Ownership of the model will be shared between the Project Company and the lenders. Exiting equity investors will also rely on the model to determine the value of their shares when looking to leave the project.

Yescombe gives a comprehensive breakdown of the inputs and outputs of the model, which are summarized here. My preference is for a simplified approach that takes in the key components while maintaining enough depth for credibility.

An important learning concept is to keep the financial model simple but with enough depth to accurately reflect your project's complexity.

Building a sound financial model is as much an art as it is a science. It must contain scientific core technical elements such as cash flows and discount factors, and art in terms of the logic behind assumptions, their place in the hierarchy and identifying the correct mitigating strategies for risk factors.

Model Inputs

The model inputs should take into account the terms set out on the project agreements and the basis for the model's assumptions. A list of model assumptions should be drawn up and any supporting documentation needs to be aligned to these. The main categories of assumptions are as follows:

1. *Macro-economic*: assumptions that are linked to wider economic factors for example, inflation rate, interest rates, commodity prices and so on;
2. *Project costs*: costs for construction, for operation and maintenance (O&M), for development and management fees. Essentially all costs that will be incurred by the Project Company need to be documented and checked for their validity;
3. *Revenues*: the Project Company's revenues, mainly driven by the amount of energy produced (or sold, if different) and the tariff of energy payments. How certain these figures are (e.g., has the PPA been signed?) will need to be clearly stated.
4. *Funding costs*: What are the interest rates being charged by the lenders? What other funding related fees will be incurred? Is there a term sheet confirming that these will be the interest rates that the Project Company should reasonably expect to pay?
5. *Accounting and taxation*: In addition to the cash flow projections, the model will need to project pro forma Profit and Loss, Balance Sheet, and Cash flow statements for the Project Company. The assumptions behind these projections should be clearly stated. Analysis around tax-related matters is important because, given the transnational nature of project finance, tax liabilities payable to the host government or other jurisdictions need to be clearly understood.

Model Outputs

Different outputs will be required from the model depending on who is looking at it. Lenders will want to see that their debt repayments are covered and that the project's income produces enough to maintain their Debt Service Coverage Ratios (DSCR). Equity investors will want to know if the projected cash flows provide their required equity IRR.

A summary sheet will simplify the many outputs of the model and should cover the following:

    i. Cash flow summary under a "Base Case" or expected set of assumptions
   ii. Equity IRR
  iii. Project IRR
   iv. Project NPV
    v. Project Company Financial Statements (Balance Sheet, P&L Cash flow Statement)
   vi. Sensitivity Analysis: which looks at scenarios other than the Base Case

The model's outputs should allow for the potential to carry out "what if" scenarios that test the impact to the model of changes to the assumptions. For example, can the project's DSCR be maintained if fuel input prices are increased by 10 percent? What happens to the project's viability if the project is delayed by a period of 6 months? The model should be tested against a reasonable selection of conceivable scenarios although project participants must be careful not to go overboard on the testing of hypothetical situations, a balance between good sense and expediency needs to be struck.

The Cash Flow Waterfall

A useful way of categorizing the cash flow related items produced by the model is to employ the cash flow waterfall.

Once a project is generating revenues, there is an order in which the various expenditure items are paid. Lenders use this when determining just how much cash there is available for the project to repay its liabilities. Figure 4.1 shows the order in which these expenditure items are paid.

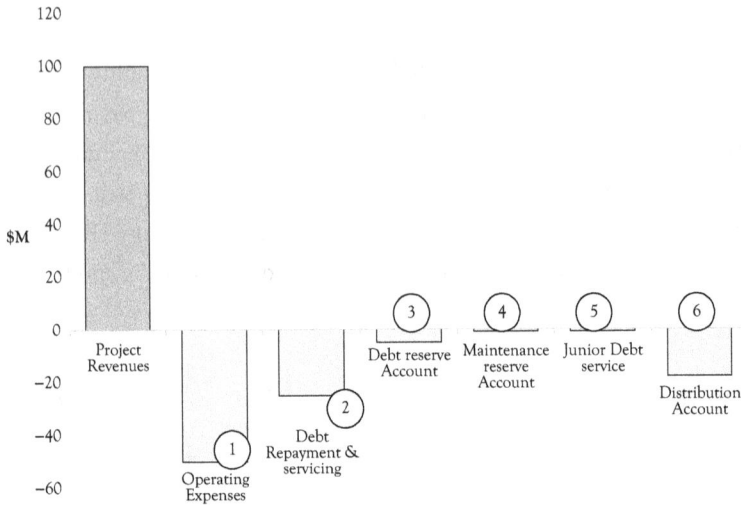

Figure 4.1 The cash flow waterfall and the hierarchy of payments

A breakdown of the hierarchy governing the expenditure items is shown below:

1. *Operating expenses*: This will cover payments to suppliers, the O&M contractor, staff costs, and so on.
2. *Debt repayment and servicing*: Repayment of
   i. loan fees, and expenses,
   ii. interest payments, and
   iii. principal
3. *Debt reserve account*: The Project Company will be obliged to fill an account for the purposes of paying future debt service during periods of lower project revenues.
4. *Maintenance reserve account*: used for the purpose of covering payments for future maintenance work.
5. *Junior debt service account*: used for repayment of subordinated debt or bondholders.
6. *Distribution account*: used for payments to the equity holders once all higher levels have been paid off.

Case Study: Project Finance Term Sheet

Table 4.1 Proposed term sheet

Proposed Term Sheet for Project Financing of 15 MW Solar Plant	
Borrower	Project Company ABC
Use of Proceeds	The construction and operation of a 15 MW solar PV farm located in West Africa
Project Cost	$20 million
Equity Contribution	Project Company will contribute 25 percent of the Project Cost on the Conversion Date
Credit Facility	Senior secured construction loan and senior secured term loan
Security	The lenders will have a senior security interest in all assets of the Project Company including plant, equipment, contracts, and bank accounts.
Construction Loan Amount	100% of the Project Cost
Conversion Date	The earlier of the Project Completion Date or one year after the Closing Date
Maturities	The Construction Loan will mature on the Conversion Date; the Term Loan will mature three years after the Conversion Date.
Repayment	The Construction Loan will be repaid from the proceeds of the Term Loan and the Equity Contribution. The Term Loan will be repaid over three years in quarterly installments to be negotiated.
Lead Arranger	A leading African Project Trade Finance Bank
Underwriting	The Lead Arranger will underwrite 100 percent of the Credit Facilities, which will be provided by a syndicate of lenders.
Underwriting fee	1.50 percent of the Construction Loan, payable on the Closing date.
Interest Rate	Construction Loan: LIBOR + 3.75percent Term Loan: LIBOR + 3.85 percent
Commitment Fee	The Borrower shall pay 0.375 percent p.a. on Undrawn Construction Loan Amounts
Drawdown	Construction Loan Amounts monthly according to an agreed plan of construction and subject to approval by the Owner's Engineer appointed by the Lead Arranger.
Distribution of Operating Cash Flows	The Borrower may distribute cash flows during the term loan period only after payment of operating expenses and debt service, funding of a 6-month debt service reserve account and subject to maintaining a Debt Service Coverage Ratio (DSCR) to be determined.
Conditions Precedent	o Technical evaluation reports by the Lenders' Owner's Engineer and other experts. o The Lead Arranger shall approve the construction budget, drawdown schedule, and financial model. o The Lead Arranger shall be satisfied that a DSCR of 2.5 can be maintained under sensitivity analysis.

The previously mentioned term sheet shown in Table 4.1, taken and redacted from a real case involving a solar PV plant in West Africa, is of particular interest on many levels.

First, note that the *Borrower* is the Project Company, an SPV created expressly for the purpose of executing and operating the project. The shareholders of the SPV are the developer and a third-party equity investor (the Sponsor). The Project Company's financing structure will therefore be made up of these two parties' equity contributions, plus the $20 million loan from the bank.

Second, *use of proceeds*—specific to project finance situations is the single project, no other purpose can be funded from this loan.

Next is *the Equity Contribution*. This loan has been structured in two parts: the first, a construction loan that will fund the construction part of the project. Once the construction has been completed, the shareholders of the SPV will be required to contribute $5 million, which will sit alongside a second loan (the term loan), for another period of three years. Such terms are common in project finance transactions; lenders view the risk profile of the construction phase differently to that of operations and so price their loans (set their interest rates) accordingly.

Now we look at *Security*; once again, with project finance situations, the Project Company has been set up for a single purpose and so it follows that the lenders' only recourse is to the assets of the Project Company. Any assets that the Sponsors possess outside of the project do not come into the picture, the bank can only lay claim on the SPV's assets. In some situations, it is not uncommon for lenders to request "Parent Guarantees" or other security from the Sponsors to provide a level of comfort if the SPV is seen as too weak to stand on its own financially. These conditions will usually be specified in the term sheet.

Underwriting: We see here that the Lead Arranger bank will usually gather a group or syndicate of other banks to fund the project. Banks use this to spread the risk of a single project across several bank balance sheets. Banks usually have a set limit on how much they can lend to a single borrower (Obligor limit).

Underwriting Fee: the Lead Arranger will claim a fee for arranging the loan. This fee will be payable at the Closing date. Note that the

Borrower is liable to pay a *Commitment Fee* for not drawing down on funds made available. Here we see the lender discouraging the Borrower from overestimating their funding requirements. Mobilization of funds for renewable energy projects takes time and effort and so banks need to be rewarded for this, regardless of whether funds are drawn down or not.

Drawdown: As we examined in the section on the financial model, the lenders will have their own in-house and external teams of experts who will scrutinize the model, the technical specifications, and the construction program of the project. Here we see the role of Owner's Engineer being applied to the Lead Arranger. Owner's Engineers can also act for the Sponsors as well.

Distribution of operating cash flows: Here we see an example of the kinds of restrictions that lenders apply in project finance. The reader would do well to cross-reference this term sheet with the section on the cash flow waterfall.

Finally, *Conditions Precedent*: We see here the stipulated due diligence that the lender needs to undertake before approving the loan. Note also the requirement that a DSCR of 2.5 be maintained under sensitivity analysis by the lender's financial modelers.

Figure 4.2 details the outputs of a real-life cash flow projection for a biomass power plant. Some figures have been slightly altered for the purposes of illustration.

First, let us look at some of the assumptions behind the figures:

1. Timeline shown is from 2020 to 2031 however the project runs until 2040.
2. Total project cost is $85 million.
3. The developer contributes $5 million in equity.
4. The developer secured further $15 million investment from an investor.
5. A commercial bank provided $65 million in debt over two years to cover the construction period.
6. The debt was charged at 5 percent interest over a period of ten years.
7. A tariff of $55/MWh over 20 years was secured for the PPA.

	Financing					Project Cash Flow							
Year	Developer Equity $M	Co-Equity investor $M	Total Dept $M	Total Dept + Equity $M	Capital Expenditure $M	Total MWh Production '000,000	Tariff per MWh $	Total Revenues $M	Operating Expenses $M	Other uses of Cash $M	Total Operating Cash Flow $M	Total Debt Service $M	Debt Service Coverage Ratio
2020	5	10	35	50	55	0	0	0	0	0	0	0	
2021	5	5	30	35	30	0	0	0	0	0	0	0	
2022						0.54	55	29.68	8.90	0.09	20.69	9.75	2.1
2023						0.77	55	42.40	12.72	6.36	23.32	9.43	2.5
2024						0.77	55	42.40	12.72	6.36	23.32	9.10	2.6
2025						0.77	55	42.40	12.72	6.36	23.32	8.78	2.7
2026						0.77	55	42.40	12.72	6.36	23.32	8.45	2.8
2027						0.77	55	42.40	12.72	6.36	23.32	8.13	2.9
2028						0.77	55	42.40	12.72	6.36	23.32	7.80	3.0
2029						0.77	55	42.40	12.72	6.36	23.32	7.48	3.1
2030						0.77	55	42.40	12.72	6.36	23.32	7.15	3.3
2031						0.77	55	42.40	12.72	6.36	23.32	6.83	3.4
	5	15	65	85	85	7.48		411.26	123.379	57.33	230.558	82.88	

Figure 4.2 Cash flow projection for biomass power plant

Looking at the table from the point of view of the lender, the last column, the DSRC, is the most important. Lenders will want to ensure that the project's cash flows are sufficient to more than cover the debt servicing and generate enough surpluses for a rainy day. A DSRC of a minimum of 2.0 (Net operating Cash flow/Debt Service) is a helpful rule of thumb for developers.

You will notice that in the first year of operations, 2022, the DSRC is at its lowest over the ten years of the debt servicing. This is explained by production of the facility beginning part way through the year and not reaching the maximum annual projections until 2023 onward. Given that debt that is drawn down accrues interest, it is vital that the project begins generating cash flows as soon as possible.

You will also notice a large leap in "Other uses of Cash" from year 2022 to 2023. This reflects clever cash flow management in the form of deferring certain expenses, where possible, to always maintain a DSCR at or above 2.0. Negotiations with suppliers such as the O&M Contractor with an aim to managing cash flow can go a long way in helping the developer secure loan funding.

The Developer's Perspective of Value

Given the detail covered earlier on the inputs and outputs of the financial model, particularly from the point of view of the lenders, let us make a little detour and look at some considerations the developer may have in this respect.

The first question—what is value? As shown previously, value can be represented by the total of the project's future earning capability as of today. As we also mentioned, different participants will have differing perceptions of value of the same project. Such as in real life where, due to the high levels of subjectivity involved in placing a value on things, different people can have wildly variant notions of the value of the same product.

Taking a first principles approach to the subject of value, I invite the reader to work with the example shown as follows, which could throw up some interesting insights. When experimenting with this topic I find that the discounted cash flow method corresponds most closely to the reality of the types of projects with which we are concerned.

An *Exercise* for Understanding Value

Key concepts: future earning capability (FEC) and lifetime expenditure (LE). In other words, how much can an asset earn over its lifetime and how much will I have to pay in order for that asset to earn its FEC?

A developer goes to a renewable convention in Singapore where a high-end solar photovoltaic (PV) panel is on display. After a detailed conversation with the vendor, the developer determines that the cost of an installed unit is $100. Unless the developer can see the value (future earnings capability as of today) of this panel as being greater than $100 plus whatever return the developer is expecting to make the whole effort worthwhile, the solar panel is of no value.

Now for a more realistic situation: an offshore wind farm. Beginning from the income side, the developer would expect to generate revenues from generating electricity from the wind turbines:

FEC: Electricity Revenues = (Output × Electricity Tariff)

Now on the lifetime expenditure side (LE):

1. *Project Development and Management Costs*
2. *Equipment*
3. *Installation and Commissioning*
4. *Operations Maintenance and Servicing*
5. *Decommissioning Costs*

A project of this level of complexity would have to have earnings projections of 20 to 25 years to make it economically viable.

For the model assumptions, try establishing a hierarchy. Those of which you are most certain go at the top and work your way down with decreasing certainty. All assumptions should have a risk factor weighted against them.

All risk factors need to be assigned to owners—those risk factors under the developer's control belong to the developer, those under the manufacturer's control to the manufacturer and so on. There will of course be those risk factors that cannot be assigned to any party for example., force majeure or residual risks.

To calculate the project's value, the cash flows need to be netted, discounted, and summed up to arrive at the project's Net Present Value (NPV).

For this exercise, keep the financial model simple. This should be used as a tool for assisting in decision making at the project's earliest stages. Besides, once investors, bankers and other experts get involved in the project there will be plenty of time for the type of model shown at the beginning of the chapter to be developed.

CHAPTER 5

The Core Principles for Developing and Financing Sustainable Energy Projects: Part III—Risk Management and Legal Aspects

After financial matters, we can now consider the final area of core principles involved in developing sustainable energy projects that is to say the legal aspects to consider and how one manages risk.

The Project Agreements

There are three main "foundation" agreements that the Project Company enters into that fit best with project finance and renewable energy projects:

 i. Offtake agreement or Power Purchase Agreement (PPA)
 ii. Availability-based contract
 iii. Concession Agreement

It is conceivable that the final contract contains provisions for all three types of agreement listed above. For example, a concession agreement granting a party the rights to build, own, operate, and transfer an energy asset can contain a PPA, which charges an Offtaker a tariff made up of charges for both capacity (or availability) and energy supplied.

Offtake agreements can take the form of take-or-pay, contracts for differences, and tolling agreements/throughput contracts. With take-or-pay, the buyer agrees to take and pay for a preagreed amount of energy, regardless of whether that energy is taken or not. The Project Company is simply obliged to deliver the energy to a specific location (e.g., the plant exit point).

A contract for difference (CfD) is designed to guarantee for the project developer a specific net price for the electricity generated where settlement prices for electricity in the market into which the electricity is sold fluctuate on a daily basis. A contract for difference will have a strike price, which sets the effective fixed net electricity price (after "differences" have been settled) that the Project Company will receive regardless of the settlement price for the period during which electricity was supplied. CfDs are used in the United Kingdom to promote low-carbon electricity generation investment but expect to see their adoption in developing markets that have to attract more investment for clean energy generation.

Throughput or tolling agreements are designed for projects where the buyer provides an input resource to the Project Company (e.g., biomass fuel), which the Project Company converts into electricity for a fee. The contract will be set up in such a way that both parties will have obligations against which they will need to perform. Such a contract will require close operational coordination between buyer and seller in order to succeed.

Availability-based contracts will contain provisions for service fees, output specification, availability requirements, and performance penalties. These put an emphasis on the Project Company's operations being able to meet the contractual requirements and somewhat shield investors from prevailing market conditions or factors external to the project's operations.

Concession agreements are an agreement between the Project Company and a Contracting Authority where the Contracting Authority confers certain rights, for example, the earning of fees or tariffs in return for designing, building, and operating a project for a period or term.

Case Study: MOU for a Concession Agreement

We can examine in more detail some of the terms of a Memorandum of Understanding (MOU), shown in Table 5.1 as a precursor to a full concession agreement on which I worked for a 15MW solar farm located in a developing country.

Let us now look at the implications detail behind each set of terms set out in the following table.

Table 5.1 Terms of a memorandum of understanding

Clause	Description
The Parties	The Contracting Authority, following its desire to promote and support the national production of electricity to increase its autonomy in the energy sector and ensure the security of supply by diversifying sources of generation that are independent of climate change notably through the construction of solar power plants in the country The Project Company that intends to invest in the construction of a 15 MW capacity solar PV power plant in the context of a Build, Own, Operate, and Transfer arrangement to sell electricity into the national grid.
Preamble	The Parties recognize that this MOU is made: In the context of reform of the electricity markets which is supported by different partners of its development and undertaken through the local electricity regulations and national law Therefore, this agreement is governed by the regulatory and statutory provisions that prevail That the Project Company declares that it is of sufficient technical and financial standing to develop the project under the terms of a BOOT agreement That the Contracting Authority has decided to award the Project Company the rights to develop, finance and construct the project as well as to preserve its ownership and operation of the solar PV power plant
Definitions	BOOT: means Build, Own, Operate, Transfer OHADA: OHADA is a system of business laws and implementing institutions adopted by 17 francophone West and Central African nations
Purpose of the Agreement	The purpose of this agreement is to award a BOOT concession for a solar PV power plant of 15MW capacity along with the requirement to construct an export cable to the high voltage network of System Operator A or the low voltage network of System Operator B.
Obligations of the Contracting Authority	The Contracting Authority commits to: Provide all approvals and permits required for the objective of constructing and operating said power plant to produce electricity Take all necessary measures to bring, in conformance to the laws in force, the contracting parties of the PPA to meet their obligations with the aim of protecting the investment of the Project Company To not carry out any expropriation, confiscation, or nationalization of the said power plant To assist the Project Company to acquire the site on which the works of construction will take place through a long lease agreement Guarantees to purchase the entire electricity production of the power plant Grants the fiscal and customs exonerations to the Project Company as a private operator, in line with the laws of the land Grants the exclusive rights to the developer to develop projects on the sites identified

(continued)

Table 5.1 (Continued)

Clause	Description
Obligations of the Project Company	The Project Company commits to: Provide all necessary documentation requested by the Contracting Authority Provide the funding for all expenses related to studies, design, and the carrying out of all construction works, both planned and otherwise and including those defined by technical experts appointed to act on the Contracting Authority's behalf Raise, at its own expense, the required financing for the Project Company to obtain the status of an independent Power Producer (IPP) acting under BOOT framework under a PPA Execute, at its own expense, the works under which the purpose of this memorandum of understanding (MOU) is defined and to confirm to both requirements for construction and the operation of said power plant under the terms of this MOU Commission the construction of the infrastructure under the laws in force Respect the provisions in the national law protecting the natural environment.
Completion of Phases	This MOU constitutes a prior approval by the Contracting Authority for a concession. The timeline for provision of the necessary documentation for studies to be carried out is as follows: Completion of a pre-FEED study within four months of the signature of this MOU Completion of a detailed FEED study within three months after approval of the pre-FEED Completion of an ESIA conforming to the prevailing legislature on the protection of the natural environment Approval of each stage shall be completed within a period of one month following receipt of the studies
Applicable Law	The laws of the host country form the legal framework under which this MOU is governed.
Confidentiality	All documentation produced within the context of this MOU shall be at the disposal to each of the Parties but remain the property of the Project Company. The Parties shall keep confidential all information obtained under the context of this MOU. The Parties agree to utilize this information only within the context of the rights and obligations set out in this MOU. Notwithstanding the above, the Project Company, for reasons pertaining to the raising of debt and equity required to realize this project, is likely to share information with third parties, be they lenders or investors, who shall preserve the confidentiality of this information. The Parties shall treat all information obtained under the auspices of the MOU as confidential and shall only use such information in the context of their obligations as set out in this agreement.

i. The Parties

It is interesting to examine the motivation of the Contracting Authority. Note that the clause highlights the Contracting Authority's desire to promote the growth of and diversify the sources of electricity production in order to secure "autonomy" and security of supply. You can rightly read between the lines that the country in question lacks enough domestic electricity production and depends heavily on imports (either of electricity or even fossil fuels) to meet its needs. Climate change is indeed mentioned but it is not the primary motivation behind the Contracting Authority's entering into this agreement with the developer.

On the other hand, the developer or Project Company's purpose seems clear—a BOOT type of arrangement to sell the electricity production of a 15MW solar PV plant.

ii. Preamble

We can pick up here the first clue that this short MOU agreement is more complex than it first appears. That clue is hidden in the following words:

> In the context of reform of the electricity markets which is supported *by different partners of its* development and undertaken through the local electricity regulations and national law.

That there is ongoing reform is not surprising for a developing country but what the developer needs to be sure of is that the cited "different partners" are on the same wavelength and stage of advancement of the Contracting Authority. It may well be that a parallel MOU with one such partner would need to be struck by the developer.

The clause seems to also reveal that at this stage of proceedings the Project Company or Sponsor has demonstrated its technical and financial capabilities to the Contracting Authority. This is not always a safe assumption to make. Unscrupulous developers, whose intent is to secure a concession under false pretenses will, often approach authorities in developing and neglected countries. Such developers do this in the hope that, having signed an agreement, they can then approach another party who is more capable of meeting the technical and financial capabilities required to carry out the obligations of the Project Company.

iii. Purpose of the Agreement

Another clue that the project will not be as straightforward as it appears is revealed here. There are two System Operators mentioned in with two connections to power grids of different specifications. The developer will need to have a good idea of which network connection is preferable and to have researched the possibilities by engaging directly with the System Operators in question.

iv. Obligations of the Contracting Authority

A few points to consider from this clause. First, the developer has to be confident of the Contracting Authority's ability to deliver all the required permits and approvals needed. Ideally, the developer will have consulted with legal experts well versed in the statutory and regulatory laws in force in the country in question.

Second, the MOU designates the Contracting Authority as a kind of referee who ensures the contracting parties of the PPA meet their respective obligations. How this will be done in practice needs to be clearly defined.

Third, in addition to its role as referee, the Contracting Authority also acts as guarantor of the PPA. Again, the developer needs to be confident that the Contracting Authority can perform the considerable obligations required of it.

Finally, the prospect of expropriation, common in some developing countries, is brought front and center among the obligations to which the Contracting Authority is expected to adhere.

v. Obligations of the Project Company

The obligations of the Project Company are straightforward and highlight what should be expected of any project developer:

(a) Have the technical and financial capabilities to deliver

(b) Work in harmony with the Contracting Authority

(c) Respect the laws in force, particularly those governing protection of the environment.

vi. Completion of Phases

This section is an interesting one and effectively summarizes a road map of how a developer brings such a project to Financial Close without taking too many risks. Essentially the developer is creating stages of government-endorsed value to the project. By this, I mean, at this stage the developer has not carried out any significant study of any kind and yet they will have signed an MOU agreement with the Contracting Authority (government agency).

So what is happening here? We see that the first phase is for a pre-FEED study to be carried out within four months of signature of the MOU. The developer will have already carried out a feasibility study that will inform much of the content of the pre-FEED so this is a good example of building a project whilst managing inherent risks.

The second phase involves progressing from pre-FEED into the more detailed FEED study. Again, much of what is performed in the pre-FEED will be integrated into the FEED document. The main difference is that the FEED will contain much more certainty on the design of the technical solution and accuracy of the costs involved. It will also serve as a crucial input into the EPC contract, which we look at later in this chapter.

Finally, the Project Company is required to deliver an ESIA subject to government approval. The vast majority of commercial lenders and pretty much all DFIs require an ESIA to be performed prior to lending into a project. Today, in our age of sustainability and the UN's SDGs, it makes perfect business sense to do so.

All these steps demonstrate the careful management of risk by the developer who works toward creating value on a systematic basis. In isolation, a pre-FEED or FEED for a project of this nature will cost several hundreds of thousands of dollars. However, a FEED document that has been approved by government and which followed a process such as that highlighted earlier will create a multiplier effect on the overall value of the project to external lenders and investors, thereby boosting the value of the project for the developer.

Such an approach is typical in jurisdictions where there is no set of regulations that govern the development of renewable energy projects. Rather, successful developers are those that can progress their way to Financial Close whilst managing the risks in as clever a manner as possible.

vii. Confidentiality

Finally, the Project Company, upon signing of this MOU and delivery of its obligations under the phasing of the project will use the

MOU to begin sounding out lenders and investors to the project. Any confidentiality clause therefore needs to give the developer the freedom to engage with third parties who may in turn contact the Contracting Authority to validate the MOU.

Terms Required in the Project Agreements

There are a number of terms that developers will need to consider when constructing agreements, whether they be the Concession Agreement or PPA:

Contract term: The developer will need to pull together a number of factors in order to arrive at the ideal period. What term are the lead arrangers quoting? Have the equity investors stated that they wish to exit within a given timeline and if so, how will that affect the payback of the overall project? How long will the equipment supplier need for lead times of delivery? Is the developer confident that the EPC contractor can deliver such a project ahead of the project completion date?

Payment Mechanism: With respect to the EPC contract, will the Contractor be paid in stages or in full at project completion? Does the Concession Agreement include payments to the Contracting Authority, which are independent of the payments received through the PPA? The developer will need to ensure that the Project Company ultimately does not bear payment risks that are not offset or mitigated in other agreements.

Compensation Events: These cover parties from the damages incurred by events usually due to the counterparty's actions. An example of this could be delays in construction meaning that the EPC Contractor would compensate the Project Company for the event. This in turn could cover the Project Company from its own obligations under the PPA to begin delivering electricity from a specific date. Compensation events serve to protect one party to one agreement from obligations in another agreement that it is unable to meet through no fault of its own.

Relief Events: From the Project Company's point of view, a Relief Event can protect it from incurring costs during a period in which revenues are not being generated. Similar to *force majeure*, which is usually covered by insurance, an example of a Relief Event could be a disruption in supplies of biomass fuel to a facility thereby preventing the Project Company from earning fees under a tolling agreement.

Step-in Rights: These could involve the investors or lenders bringing in their own management teams to operate the Project Company, in the event that the developer/sponsor is unable for whatever reason to do so. Step-in rights of this nature will feature in the loan and shareholder agreements.

Termination: Termination of an agreement prior to the end of its normal term is an outcome that needs to be seriously considered by the developer. Should the Project Company default on either the PPA or Concession Agreement, or both, it may involve payment of compensation to counterparties and transfer of the project to the counterparty. Termination clauses can come loaded with payable sums, which adds to the burden of default. From the Project Company's perspective, a large termination payment in the event that the Contracting Authority or Buyer of the PPA defaults can go a long way in attracting prospective investors, especially where the counterparty has a track record of default which is not unheard of in developing countries.

Force majeure: Events such as war or terrorism could lead to an agreement being terminated. In such a case, the repayment of outstanding debt or the making whole of the investors. Partial Risk Guarantees such as those proved by the like of MIGA offer the protection needed in cases like this.

Change of Ownership: Either the Contracting Authority or lenders and investors may wish to restrict the developer's ability to exit a project before a prescribed time period. This is particularly the case where the Project Company's operating abilities rely heavily on the developer, who may have intentions to sell out early and move on to the next project.

Other Project Agreements

In addition to the aforementioned foundation agreements there are other contracts the developer will need to negotiate and integrate into the project documentation.

EPC Contract: Developers will usually opt for a lump sum or turnkey agreement to have certainty over the construction costs. Contractors, for their part, will "bake" in a premium to the quoted amount, which is designed, from their perspective, to provide a buffer from the additional risk that such a contract brings.

Alongside the legal boilerplate terms such as relief events, termination and performance bonds, the EPC contract will depend heavily on the terms of reference defined in the FEED documentation. In some projects I have come across, the EPC Contractor is also the party that produced the FEED document. Developers employ such an approach to save on costs or build on a strong working relationship with a Contractor.

O&M Contract: This contract will govern work performed by the entity that ensures that the plant performs to the expected levels throughout the life or the project. The scope of services will include planning, mobilization and operations and the fees paid to the Contractor will usually form a sizeable portion of the project's Operating Expenses.

It is therefore important that an O&M Contractor with a track record of performance, preferably within the host country, is selected for the role. Performance can be measured with preagreed Key Performance Indicators (KPIs) with penalties and incentives employed to generate the desired outcomes. Process-heavy energy facilities such as biomass plants demand a different and, at times, much more demanding operating ability than wind or solar PV plants.

Fuel Supply Contract: For biomass projects that depend on a third party to supply an input fuel there are many factors to consider. These include fixed and/or variable supply elements where a supplier is obliged to provide a fixed portion, as a minimum, and a variable amount on top of that, if their supply chain permits it. In such a contract, the buyer may find it preferable to have variability on the pricing to offset the adverse impact of variable pricing on operating expenses. For example, the buyer may wish to pay a certain price for the fixed portion and a lower price, on a sliding scale, for any additional amounts attributable to the variable portion.

Fuel Supply Agreement   Tolling Agreement
                                          Power Purchase Agreement

Figure 5.1 Examples of "upstream" and "downstream" contracts

As stated previously, the Project Company will need to ensure that risks and obligations set out in the supply agreement are coordinated with those in the downstream tolling or power purchase agreements Figure 5.1 illustrates examples of both downstream and upstream contracts.

Main Risks and Risk Allocation

The correct allocation of risk will make the difference in achieving Financial Close. The myriad of stakeholders, phases, and variables involved in developing a project, even in developed markets, means that lenders and investors will want to make sure that risks are correctly allocated and that the risk owners are capable of assuming their respective risks.

This will involve much negotiation at every turn because, naturally, no one wants to take on any risk that they do not have to. Often counterparties, as an opening gambit, will dispatch a draft agreement where the other party is assumed to take on a greater amount of risk than they will. In developing markets where there is much uncertainty and little depth in financial or insurance markets to mitigate risk, the challenge is even greater. Taking the MOU used in our Case Study in the section on Project Agreements one can easily guess, given the relatively soft obligations demanded of the Project Company, that the original draft was prepared by the developer.

First, let us look at a summary of the four main risk categories that are faced by developers in a project finance situation:

1. *Project risks*: Risks that are in inherent in the project itself, or the market in which it operates.
   - *Commercial viability*: Can the project, following the technical, legal, and financial groundwork be commercially

feasible? The Offtaker's ability to pay needs to be examined as well as other factors.

- *Construction risk*: The main driver is to consider whether the EPC Contractor can deliver the project on time, within budget and to specifications. Under a fixed price agreement, what provisions are made for unforeseen changes to project specification or delays? Other aspects related to this include the mitigation of delays to completion of the project and whether the Project Company and or the EPC Contractor can absorb this. With respect to issues arising from the site and consents we saw earlier, in the MOU for the Concession Agreement, that the Contracting Authority would take responsibility for obtaining the necessary consents. In the event that these were needed, can the Contracting Authority be relied upon to deliver in a timely fashion?

- *Revenue risk*: What are the risks behind the Project Company not achieving the projected revenues? Is there a price risk (in the case that the expected prices are not met)? What about volume risk (where projected volumes are overestimated because of weather or even miscalculations at the design stage?)

- *Operating risk*: Risks that arise from the nonperformance of the technology or shortcomings in the O&M contractor's performance need to be analyzed here. For example, in the event the O&M contractor incurs a penalty is it able to pay? This is where engaging an O&M Contractor with a track record for the technology and in the host country is essential. Such an O&M Contractor, however, will likely charge more for their service, which will impact the operating expenses.

- *Input supply risk*: For a biomass or energy plant that depends on a supply chain this risk is important to mitigate. Term and reliability of supplies, quality of product, and pricing are key risks to note in negotiating a fuel supply contract.

2. *Macroeconomic risks*: Relate to external economic effects not directly related to the project (i.e., inflation, interest rates, and currency-exchange rates).

- *Interest rate risk*: Developing markets tend to have high local interest rates that the Project Company will have to absorb. On the one hand, the Project Company will have to repay interest at a rate that will need to be indexed to the price the Project Company earns from the Offtaker. PPAs and other agreements are often linked to the prevailing consumer price index. It should also be noted here that once the lenders' funds are drawn down at Financial Close, they will begin to accrue interest which builds up during a period when the project is not generating income. The Project Company (more specifically its owners) are expected to assume this risk.
- *Inflation risk*: Inflation risk is normally controlled by having fixed contract prices for either construction or operating expenses. Including the risk of inflation in all Project Agreements, best addresses this.
- *Foreign exchange "forex" risk*: For projects in developing countries, the subject of forex risk depends largely on the currency in which the lenders will lend to the project. Developers, especially foreign-based ones, will likely have one base currency. Suppliers located in different countries may have another. All project participants may be asked to deal in U.S. dollars, which for some countries brings considerable risk. It is for the developer to decide on which currency is best for developing the project and to structure the project accordingly. The involvement of DFIs will mean U.S. dollars will feature in some shape or form in the project. If the Project Company earns its revenues in another currency, then the developer will need to hedge the Project Company's currency exposure in the currency swap markets. Many DFIs are experienced in dealing with this kind of scenario and will provide their own instruments to cover this.

3. *Regulatory and political risks*: Risks brought about by changes in law, or risks that relate to the effects of expropriation or war.
   - *Change of law risk*: Many developing countries do not have regulatory frameworks in place that govern the development

of renewable energy projects. This leaves developers exposed to the risk of laws being changed that are to the detriment of the Project Company. Developers have to be astute and use their judgment in managing this risk and aim for realistic, long-term returns on their investment. As we saw in the case study, having a Contracting Authority or Host Government commit to safeguarding investment in the project goes a long way in mitigating this risk. It is not realistic to expect a government to commit to not changing a law because changes in government can occur over the lifetime of a project. Project developers should seek to transcend political whims by promoting projects that adhere to the UN's SDGs.

The Developer's Risk Matrix

As demonstrated earlier, it should be evident that developers need to identify, quantify, and then allocate (where possible) the risks under each of the aforementioned categories to the various project participants, including insurance or risk guarantee providers such as DFIs who are particularly useful in dealing with the third category.

There is no magic bullet however and so residual risks will remain. The compensation for enduring these residual risks is reflected in the returns paid back to the project's equity investors. It makes little sense to expect all risks to be eliminated and most project participants, including Contracting Authorities and Offtakers, appreciate that the Project Company has a limited ability to absorb all of the risks within the project.

Project participants should also be mindful that, when one party seeks to offload a risk to another that the second party will seek to protect themselves within the contract. This will be done either by increasing the tariff charged (e.g., in a tolling agreement or PPA) or charging more to perform a service as is the case that EPC Contractors do when requested to provide a fixed price for an EPC contract. Adding these "inflated" costs to the substantial costs that come with taking out comprehensive insurance coverage for political risks, can very easily turn a viable project unviable.

Every developer should therefore have a risk allocation matrix, which will foster a deep understanding of the arrangements that will be required to make the project ultimately bankable. The risk allocation matrix will help in the process of putting in place all the contractual agreements needed to deliver the project. It is a useful exercise for the developer to construct the matrix at the very early stages of the project and set out what mitigations you will employ for each of the risks listed in the matrix below.

This matrix looks at the typical set of risks involved in a generic renewable energy project and details how these risks should be managed. Starting with the assumption that the output of the plant will be sold to a state-owned utility, we can further assume that:

1. Project will be developed and operated by private entity (BOO).
2. Developer will be responsible for associated electricity transmission infrastructure.
3. Developer has identified the site on which the project is to be located.

The key risks associated with a project of this nature are:

1. *Resource risk*: Cost or availability of equipment will weigh heavily on the chosen EPC contractor. You will need to find a contractor who will have the depth and experience needed to mitigate the risk associated with this.
2. *Performance or price risk*: State-owned utilities in developing countries may not have strong credit ratings. This will need to be backed up by government or international credit guarantees.
3. *Political risk*: While insurance for government expropriation and other related risks are available, these can come at a high cost, which will need to be met by the project's payback.

In order to mitigate the risks present in the project, the developer will need to make use of contractual agreements, financial instruments, and partners. Putting the required mitigants in place will take time and effort, thereby adding to the urgency of putting together a risk allocation matrix as early as possible. Table 5.2 is an example of such a risk matrix.

The counterparties that are referenced in the matrix are listed as follows:

1. *The developer*: The main actor who bears ultimate responsibility of ensuring that all risks are correctly allocated and mitigated.

2. *The Offtaker*: In this case, the state-owned utility that is responsible for paying the agreed tariff over the duration of the PPA.

3. *Commercial lenders*: Lending into a project with so many dependencies leads to extensive risk mitigation wrapped into the financing agreements.

4. *Equity investors*: Investors will expect the developer to have done their homework on risk mitigation.

5. *Design engineers*: Responsible for producing the FEED documentation but usually do not hold any liability should their design "fail" after having been initially accepted by the EPC contractor. At any rate, proving that a design has failed ex-post is a costly and time-consuming effort.

6. *Consultants*: Those responsible for producing the feasibility studies, the ESIA, and other supporting studies. Not given usually to taking on any risks associated with their work and so the developer pays for, and ultimately takes responsibility for, the results.

7. *The EPC Contractor*: Responsible for delivering the energy asset in conformance with the design specifications set out in the FEED. As mentioned earlier will need to have capability to mitigate the multiple risks involved in taking on an EPC contract.

8. *Multilateral Investment Guarantee Agency* (*MIGA*): An IFC institution that provides insurance covering political and other risks in emerging markets.

The project documentation that is referenced in the matrix is listed below:

1. *The Power Purchase Agreement* (PPA): Usually will be "take or pay," which means that the Offtaker will pay an agreed amount to the seller regardless of whether the electricity is used or not. This is to ensure that the project's financing is covered through the duration of the PPA's term.

2. *Front-end Engineering and Design* (FEED): Concept design and detailed engineering performed by engineers and designers. This document will be a fundamental element of the procurement of the EPC contractor and eventual drafting of the EPC contract.

3. *Feasibility studies*: Prior to any detailed engineering work, the project will have to be independently verified as viable in all aspects including technically, commercially, financially, and environmentally.

4. *Environmental and Social Impact Assessment* (ESIA): A key agreement without which lenders and investors will be unable to fund the project.

5. *The EPC contract*: Entered into with the EPC contractor, this agreement will set out the obligations of the contractor in delivering an energy asset that will perform to the level required to ensure a return on investment for the project.

6. *The loan facility*: Agreement reached between the project developer and the lenders.

7. *Equity Investment Agreement*: An agreement covering the terms of an equity investment between the developer and equity investors.

8. *O&M Agreements*: Covers the operations of the plant once it has been commissioned.

Table 5.2 Exemplar risk matrix

	Owner	Type	Description	Mitigation	Documentation/ Agreement
1.	Developer	Site	The risk of acquiring title to the project site, the selection of that site and its geophysical conditions. Other considerations that affect this include planning permission, access rights, indigenous land rights, archaeology, and pollution.	The developer should undertake detailed ground, geotechnical, environmental, and social assessments/surveys and should disclose such information to the relevant authorities where necessary. The developer should ensure that it has a complete understanding of the risks involved in securing the site and the site constraints that will affect the construction and operation of the facility.	Feasibility Studies ESIA
2.	Developer	Environmental and social	The risk of environmental conditions affecting the project and the subsequent risk of damage to the environment or local communities.	The developer should ensure that any contractor complies with any applicable permits and consents by way of the inclusion of corresponding obligations in the EPC and O&M agreements.	ESIA EPC Contract O&M Contract
3.	Developer	Design	The risk that the project has not been designed adequately for the purpose required.	The developer should promote a collaborative environment at design and engineering so that there is cooperation to ensure an appropriate risk allocation for design responsibility. Consultant engineers and the EPC contractor will need clear lines of communication and transparency in order to ensure that the design of the plant is successfully implemented.	FEED

(continued)

4.	EPC contractor	Construction	Can include risk arising from labor disputes, project interface, and project management. Defective labor, material, and cost overruns where no compensation/relief event applies.	The developer should address this by passing through obligations to the EPC contractor and the management services contractor (if applicable). Adequate insurance will cover the transportation of the valuable equipment from overseas and will be required by both the developer and the EPC contractor.	EPC Contract Insurance
5.	EPC Contractor	Completion	The risk of not commissioning the asset on time and on budget and the consequences of missing either of those two criteria.	Generally, the developer should pass risks associated with delay in achieving commercial operation on to the EPC contractor to minimize potential impact on the project's financials. Turnkey or "lump sum" EPC contracts are employed so that the EPC contractor has to take on the risk of time delays to delivery of the project. EPC Contracts will often contain liquidated damages and financial penalties and can assist in enforcing construction deadlines. Ensuring that the construction program has sufficient margin for all critical stages and that parties are incentivized to work together to achieve the common deadlines may be more effective strategies.	EPC Contract
6.	EPC Contractor	Performance/ price	The risk that the asset is not able to achieve the output specification metrics at the price or cost of doing so.	The developer should ensure that appropriate guaranteed levels be included in the construction and operations contracts with damages payable by the EPC contractor for a failure to reach those guaranteed levels.	EPC Contract

(continued)

Table 5.2 (Continued)

	Owner	Type	Description	Mitigation	Documentation/ Agreement
7.	EPC Contractor	Resource/input	The risk that the supply of inputs or resources required for the construction of the project is interrupted or the cost increases	Lump sum contracts can mitigate this risk to the developer although contractors usually respond to this by increasing their fee.	EPC Contract
8.	Offtaker	Demand	The availability, by both volume and quality of resource or inputs, to a project; or the demand for the product or service of a project by consumers/users.	Take-or-Pay contract structure must be adopted. The developer should seek for the offtake agreement to provide returns for availability (capacity payments) and supply (energy payments).	PPA
9.	O&M Contractor	Maintenance	The risk of maintaining the asset to the appropriate standards and specifications for the life of the project. Increased maintenance costs due to increased volumes, incorrect estimates and cost overruns.	The developer must ensure that the specifications set out in the FEED are achievable and agreed with the EPC Contractor and, following that, taken on as obligations by the O&M contractor. It is usually preferable that the same party that delivered the EPC contract will execute the O&M, thereby ensuring no performance or specification gaps exist between construction and operations.	O&M
10.	Developer	Disruptive technology	The risk that a new, emerging technology unexpectedly displaces established technology used in solar PV projects.	This is usually a risk that the developer has to bear, although some may oblige contractors and manufacturers to upgrade technology during the procurement process.	EPC Contract

11.	Lenders	Early termination	The risk of a project being terminated before the expiry of time and the monetary consequences of such a termination.	It is important that the developer understands that commercial lenders understandably devote a lot of time toward mitigating early termination. The PPA should ensure termination clauses are not triggered lightly and that there is adequate provision for remedy of defaults and dispute resolution. Lenders usually cover themselves by invoking "step-in" rights that allow them to deal directly with the Offtaker should the developer be in default. Lenders can ultimately seek to bring in a third party to execute the contract should the developer fail.	PPA Lending Agreements
12.	Developer	Exchange and interest rate	The risk of currency fluctuations and/or the interest rate over the life of a project.	The developer should put hedging arrangements in place. The EPC contractor should also seek to hedge any foreign currency exposure it may have in relation to foreign currency imports.	Financial instruments
13.	Developer	Insurance	The risk that insurance for particular risks is, or becomes, unavailable.	As part of the feasibility study, the developer should consider whether insurance might become unavailable for it, given the location and other factors relevant to the project.	Feasibility studies
14.	Developer	Inflation	The risk that the costs of the project increase more than expected.	The developer should hedge this risk through appropriate financial instruments. The EPC contractor should also seek to hedge any foreign currency exposure it may have in relation to foreign currency imports.	PPA EPC Contract O&M Contract Financial instruments

(continued)

Table 5.2 (Continued)

	Owner	Type	Description	Mitigation	Documentation/ Agreement
15.	Shared	*Force majeure*	The risk that unexpected events occur that are beyond the control of the parties and delay or prohibit performance.	All contractual agreements will cite the events that fall under *force majeure*, thereby allowing all contractual parties to share such risk. It is the responsibility of the developer that *force majeure* clauses across all agreements are in synchronicity and that *force majeure* in, say, the O&M agreement does match the *force majeure* as defined in the PPA or lending agreements. Insurance instruments such as those provided by MIGA can cover much of what could be defined as *force majeure* including war, terrorism, and civil disobedience.	Insurance PPA EPC Contract O&M Contract Lending Agreements Investment Agreements
16.	Shared	Political	The risk of government intervention, discrimination, seizure, or expropriation of the project.	Although MIGA can cover government expropriation, this can add significantly to the project costs, thereby adding pressure on the tariff to be paid in the PPA. The developer should work with the host government to ensure other government departments are in line with the project. This will require active stakeholder engagement and management as described in the section on measuring sustainable return. The developer should also verify that investors, commercial lenders, and other partners also separately take out insurance to cover themselves.	Insurance

| 17. | Developer | Regulatory | The risk of law changing and affecting the ability of the project to perform and the price at which compliance with law can be maintained.
Change in taxation | The developer will need to ensure that the PPA makes provision for ensuring regulatory changes do not negatively influence the financial viability of the project.
As part of its stakeholder management strategy, the developer should work with the host government to ensure various government departments keep the project in mind when passing new laws. | PPA |
| 18. | Developer | Strategic | Change in shareholding of the developer of the SPV.
Conflicts of interest between shareholders of the SPV. | The Offtaker will ensure in the PPA that it is protected from such risk by restricting the developer's ability to change shareholding for a period.
The developer should bear this in mind for any future exit strategy | PPA |

Source: https://ppp-risk.github.org/

CHAPTER 6

Frontier and Emerging Markets: How They Differ

In essence, developing countries (emerging and frontier markets) are distinguished by higher perceived levels of risk. According to the World Bank's International Finance Corporation (IFC), typical characteristics of such markets include difficult conditions for private investment, lack of services, lack of jobs, and higher rates of poverty.

As a developer, you will be faced with specific challenges that you would not encounter in developed markets such as:

1. Lack of regulation around tariffs
2. Lack of technical understanding
3. Difficulty in procuring technical equipment required
4. Lack of local financing options
5. Low level of interest from venture capitalists or other early-stage funders

Faced with the above, most individuals would not attempt to develop projects in frontier or emerging markets; however, you have read this far, for a reason. Below we will look at a group of developing countries that are making enormous progress in growing their renewable energy sectors. We will look at what their factors for success are, and what these countries have done to address the challenges faced by developers.

The good news is that there is increasing recognition that more investment needs to flow into developing countries. Furthermore, the imperative to transition the global economy to low carbon creates a unique opportunity for specialists in renewable energy to enter markets that have a need and a willingness to adopt more renewables.

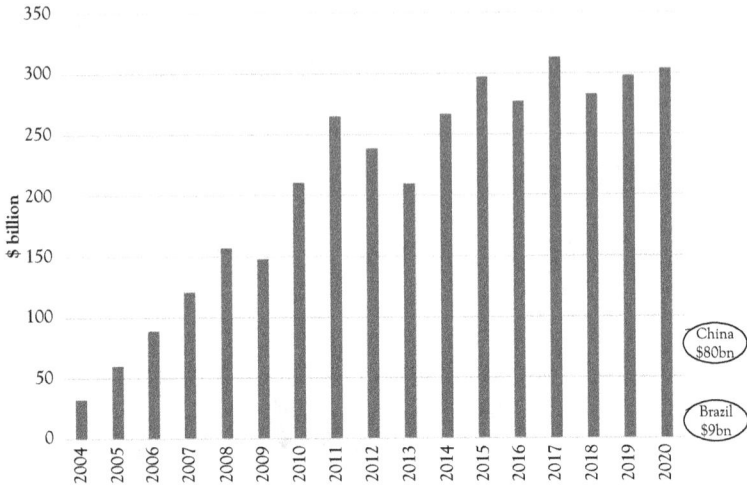

Figure 6.1 Global renewable energy investment

Source: BloombergNEF.

According to BloombergNEF's New Energy Outlook 2020, global annual renewable energy investment reached $300 billion in 2020. Of this amount, China alone made up almost a quarter with around $80 billion invested in renewable energy. While China, as developing countries go, may be an outlier; the general consensus is that growth in the adoption of renewables in developing countries will ramp up considerably over the next 10 years. Figure 6.1 shows the levels of investment globally.

According to the UN Environment Programme, investment in renewable energy capacity in developing countries has outstripped that in developed countries consistently since 2014. Outside of China and India, this figure reached $47.5 billion in 2018. For developing countries excluding China and India, investment in renewables capacity increased by 22 percent from 2017 to 2018.

With this context in mind, which are the developing markets with growth potential and, equally importantly, why do they offer such potential? The answer to the latter will assist you in knowing which indicators to look out for when seeking growth opportunities in other markets.

In terms of abundance of renewable potential, the Middle East and Africa are sure to be next in line to follow the likes of China, India, and

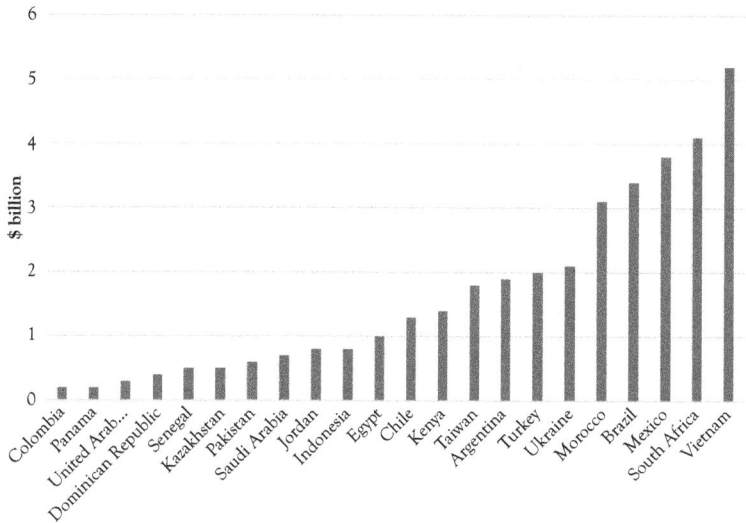

Figure 6.2 Renewable energy capacity investment 2018

Source: UN Environment, Frankfurt-School-UNEP, BloombergNEF.

Brazil. UN Environment has reported renewables investment in both regions reached $16.1 billion in 2018, of which $10.1 billion was in solar. The same period saw a fivefold increase in wind investment.

Figure 6.2 shows the amount of investment in renewable energy for a selection of developing countries. The big players here are Vietnam, South Africa, Mexico, Brazil, and Morocco whose combined investment in renewables was around 7 percent of global investment in 2018. Let us look behind those figures to build up a picture of what went on in those countries.

Vietnam

The United States Energy Information Administration offers a good starting point for developers researching prospective emerging markets. One can access base data covering the entire energy portfolio of a country, Source the production and consumption data, including the in-country energy sources and tap into analysis on the past, present and future outlook. Table 6.1 provides high level primary energy data and Figure 6.3 breaks down the breakdown of renewables for Vietnam.

Table 6.1 Vietnam Primary energy data 2018

Total Energy 2018 (quadrillion Btu)	All sources	Nuclear, renewables, and other	Renewables Generation
Production	2.732	0.768	28%
Consumption	3.717	0.773	

Source: EIA.

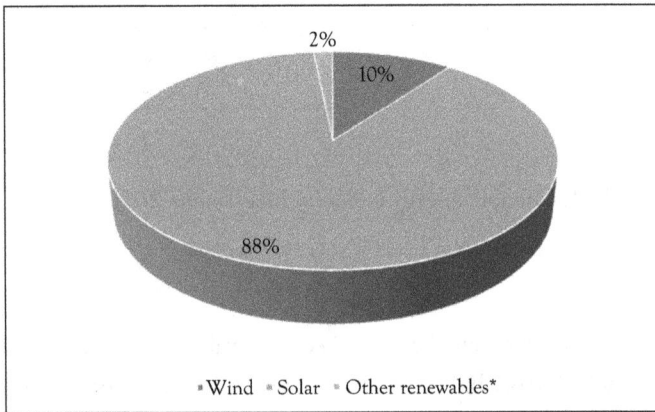

* Includes electricity generated from: geothermal, biomass and other sources of renewable energy (not already itemised).

Figure 6.3 Vietnam renewable energy generation 2019

Source: bp Statistical Review 2020.

By analyzing data from multiple sources, we can discern a direction of travel for development of renewable energy projects in a given country. This analysis can assist greatly in the decision-making process of whether to begin in-country development. What do we know about the $5.2 billion that was invested in 2018? Research by UNEP shows that $44.6 billion of that amount came from solar projects, with 10 solar PV projects of at least 100 MW reaching financial close that year. The rest of the investment ($599 million) came from investments in wind energy.

Behind this project development activity lay a renewable energy feed-in tariff of 9.35 U.S. cents per kWh for 20 years.

Table 6.2 Vietnam renewable energy projects

Project	Technology	Capacity (MW)	Estimated cost ($million)	Cost ($million/ MW)
Tieng Reservoir Tay Ninh Plant	Solar PV	420	402	0.96
Hong Phong Binh Thuan Bac Binh	Solar PV	351	326	0.93
Cong Ly Bac Lieu	Offshore wind	142	392	2.76

Source: UNEP. Author's analysis.

The last column of Table 6.2 is particularly interesting for the developer; the cost per MW of developing offshore wind is three times that of solar, yet these are projects that ultimately produce the same commodity—electricity. Developers, depending on their own competitive advantage among other factors, will want to understand what the relative costs are of developing renewable projects using different technologies in different jurisdictions.

South Africa

South Africa's electricity generation portfolio has, historically, been dominated by coal-fired power plants, reflecting the country's standing as holding the world's tenth largest amount of recoverable coal reserves. Table 6.3 provides high level primary energy data and Figure 6.4 the renewables generation mix for South Africa.

So what is the latest we know about renewable projects in the country? We know that of the $4.1 billion of investment it attracted in 2018, wind farm investments made up $2.7 billion and solar $1.3 billion. Standing behind much of this project activity is Eskom, the country's electricity utility.

Developers signed PPAs with Eskom, having bid for capacity through renewable energy auctions. This is a feature in more sophisticated markets, where developers are invited to bid for a set capacity, for example 100 MW with an associated tariff and term that they are willing to offer

Table 6.3 South Africa Primary energy data 2018

Total Energy 2018 (quadrillion Btu)	All sources	Nuclear, renewables, and other	Renewables Generation
Production	5.637	0.218	4%
Consumption	3.854	0.216	

Source: EIA.

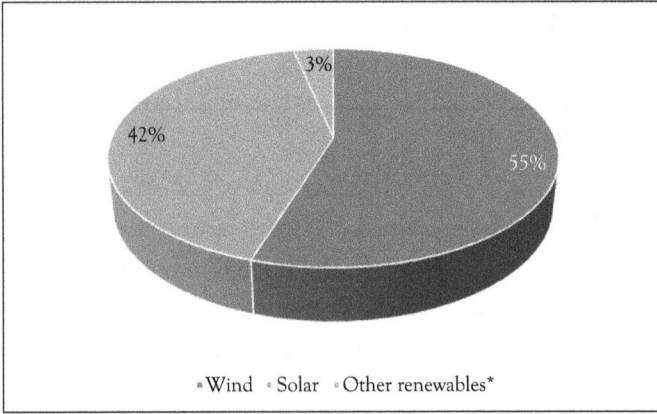

Figure 6.4 South Africa Renewable energy generation 2019

Source: bp Statistical Review 2020.

the buyer, in this case Eskom. The buyer (Offtaker) then assesses these bids and decides on which to accept. Upon acceptance, the developer now has to go and develop the project, raising the necessary financing and other resources required.

You will find that developers with a large internal capacity of development resources are the few capable of participating in such auctions. Large international utilities like Engie (France) and ENEL Green Power (Italy), along with renewable project development specialists like Scatec ASA (Norway), scour the globe in search of developing markets in which they can bring their expertise to bear. Table 6.4 shows a sample of such projects in South Africa.

Of further interest to note is the relatively higher cost per MW compared to Vietnam. This could be due to a number of factors including different tariff structures, labor costs, taxes, and regulatory requirements.

Table 6.4 South Africa renewable energy projects

Project	Technology	Capacity (MW)	Estimated cost ($million)	Cost ($million/MW)
Enel Green Power	Wind	704	1,300	1.84
Scatec Solar	Solar PV	258	396	1.53

Source: UNEP.Author's analysis.

Table 6.5 Mexico Primary energy data 2018

Total Energy 2018 (quadrillion Btu)	All sources	Nuclear, renewables, and other	Renewables Generation
Production	6.285	0.625	10%
Consumption	7.997	0.657	

Source: EIA.

Mexico

Mexico is a large producer of petroleum products that has stated ambitions to increase its renewable generation capacity in the coming years. Table 6.5 gives a breakdown of the country's primary energy data and we see from Figure 6.5 that almost half of its renewable portfolio is made up of wind power, which reflects the attractiveness of the market to wind energy developers.

Mexico is a regional leader for renewable energy investment and in 2018, the Secretaría de Energía (SENER) announced that over 1,100 billion pesos would be invested in clean energy generation up to the year 2035. Table 6.6 lists a selection of recent renewable projects.

Brazil

Brazil is the largest energy market of the developing countries in our selection. Furthermore, as we can see in Table 6.7 and Figure 6.6, its renewable energy sector is many times larger than the others. What is behind these numbers?

A big explanation behind the statistics is the country's very high hydro-electric power production numbers. That being the case, according to bp's

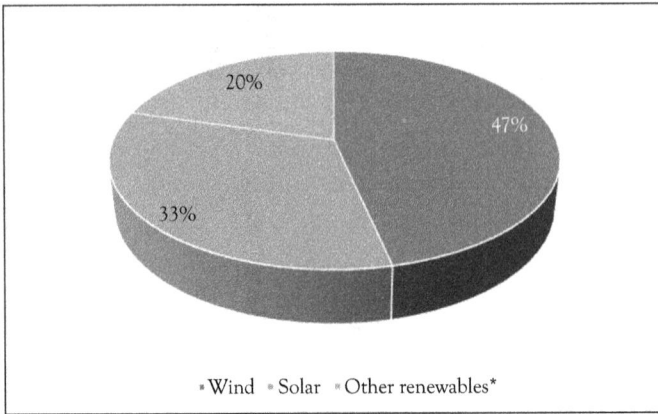

Figure 6.5 Mexico Renewable energy generation 2019

Source: bp Statistical Review 2020.

Table 6.6 Mexico renewable energy projects

Project	Technology	Capacity (MW)	Estimated cost ($million)	Cost ($million/MW)
Acciona and Tuto Puerto Libertad PV plant	Solar PV	493	404	0.82
EnerAB Mesa La Paz	Wind	306	405	1.32

Source: UNEP.Author's analysis.

Table 6.7 Brazil Primary energy data 2018

Total Energy 2018 (quadrillion Btu)	All sources	Nuclear, renewables, and other	Renewables Generation
Production	12.148	5.491	45%
Consumption	12.759	4.804	

Source: EIA.

Statistical Review for 2020, the combined share of hydro and renewables will grow from 52 to 80 percent of the entire energy mix.

Yet the 2018 investment of $3.4 billion was 44 percent lower than that in the previous year. Wind energy investment suffered the largest

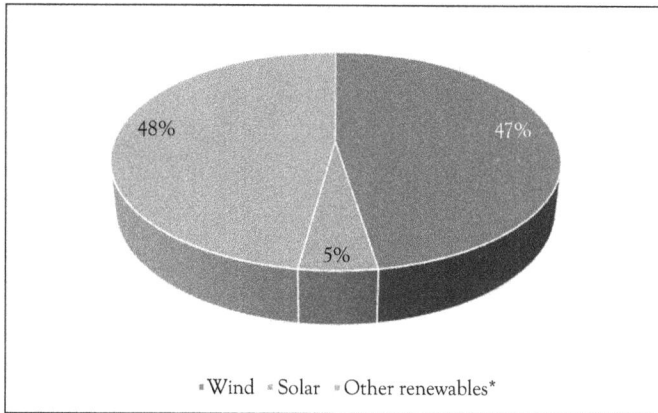

Figure 6.6 Brazil Renewable energy generation 2019

Source: bp Statistical Review 2020.

Table 6.8 Brazil renewable energy projects

Project	Technology	Capacity (MW)	Estimated cost ($million)	Cost ($million/MW)
Enel Sao Goncalo PV	Solar PV	388	390	1.01

Source: UNEP. Author's analysis.

Table 6.9 Morocco Primary energy data 2018

Total Energy 2018 (quadrillion Btu)	All sources	Nuclear, renewables, and other
Production	0.063	0.059
Consumption	0.85	0.071

Source: EIA.

drop (61 percent) contributing $1.3 billion, while solar attracted $1.8 billion in investment. Why did this fall occur? Research shows that no auctions for new generating capacity took place between November 2015 and December 2017. Given the nature of the projects in question, with long lead times for development and construction, developers must be

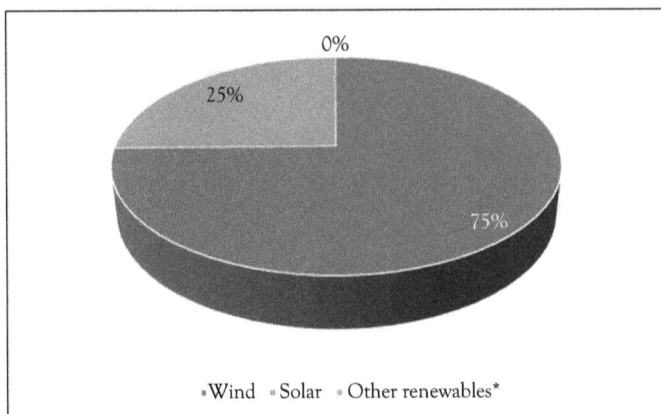

Figure 6.7 *Morocco Renewable energy generation 2019*

Source: bp Statistical Review 2020.

Table 6.10 *Morocco renewable energy projects*

Project	Technology	Capacity (MW)	Estimated cost ($million)	Cost ($million/ MW)
Noor Solar complex Ouar- zazate	Concentrating Solar Power (CSP) and Solar PV	580	9,000	15.52
Khalladi Wind Farm Tangiers	Wind	120	170	1.42
Midelt, Tanger, JbelLahdid, Tiskrad, and Boujdour*	Wind	850	1,220	1.44
NOORm Midelt PV	Solar PV	800	2,400	3

Source: UNEP.Author's analysis.
Five projects to be delivered by a consortium including Nareva (Morocco), Enel Green Power (Italy),and Siemens Wind Power (Germany)

wary of not placing too many of their development eggs in one basket. If you are going to pursue projects in developing markets, having a geo- graphically diversified portfolio makes sense. Table 6.8 provides a sum- mary of a recent major renewable project.

Morocco

The data presented in Table 6.9 is slightly different from that presented for other countries. This is because Morocco produces very little of its own energy resources and therefore has to import most of its energy. In 2017, according to the EIA, 80 percent of the country's electricity was produced from fossil fuels with wind, solar, and hydro making up 15 percent. Figure 6.7 provides a breakdown of the country's renewable mix.

The country sees the expansion of the renewables market as a way out of its heavy dependence on hydrocarbon imports. The state utility ONEE is aiming for 52 percent of the country's electricity needs to be met by wind and solar generation by 2030. In 2018 alone, solar capacity tripled to 711 MW.

The total investment in renewables for 2018 was $3.1 billion, with $2.6 billion in solar financing and $439 million for wind. As far as developing countries go, it is an attractive prospect for developers.

Thanks to the eye-catching capital cost of $15.52 million/MW, Table 6.10 throws up an interesting technology that we have not looked at so far—Concentrated Solar Power (CSP). CSP employs mirrors to concentrate heat from the sun's rays, heat that is then used to drive steam turbines. Thanks to thermal storage, CSP can provide round-the-clock electricity unlike solar PV.

From our analysis of the five leading developing countries for renewable energy investment, we can draw some important lessons as to why these markets have attracted, and continue to attract, major investment from developers:

1. **Feed-in tariffs or other incentives (e.g., capacity auctions)**
   Feed-in tariffs offer a guaranteed price for a project's energy output, which is the ideal for most developers. Capacity auctions are an innovation that ensures the Offtaker receives a range of bids under competitive conditions, which will ideally allow the "cheapest" project to win. Electricity customers are, in theory, guaranteed the lowest price possible for producing that renewable electricity, which is of crucial importance for countries with significant population segments living at or below the poverty line.

2. **Creditworthy offtaker**

The credit-worthiness of the Offtaker is fundamental to the success of a project financing. In some cases, the host government has to step in to provide additional financial heft to a state utility's balance sheet if they hope to attract renewable energy investment. The countries we have looked at have all addressed this issue and so this should be a key point when evaluating a potential market.

3. **Set targets for generation mix**

All of the countries we looked at had set targets for increasing their proportion of renewables at some point up to the year 2050. This is an encouraging sign for developers because it shows that the host government has at least staked its reputation toward promoting renewables. However, the setting of targets needs to go hand in hand with the other factors listed here.

4. **Open acknowledgment of cost-effectiveness of renewables.**

All of the countries that we looked at are endowed with abundant renewable resources, be it wind, solar, and even geothermal (in the case of Mexico). More and more governments are waking up to the fact that the levelized cost of renewable technologies, in particular solar PV, onshore and offshore wind, has come down so far over the past decade that for many countries renewable technologies offer the cheapest option for producing more energy.

Why Do Developing Markets Find Project Finance Interesting?

As we have seen previously, the benefits of project financing to developing countries and their agencies are numerous:

- Lower product or service cost;
- Additional investment in public infrastructure;
- Lower project cost—the private sector can often build and run such investments more cost-effectively than the public sector;
- Third-party due diligence and the promotion of transparency;
- Additional inward investment; project finance opens up new opportunities for infrastructure investment, as it can be used to create inward investment that would not otherwise occur;

- Financial-market development, as typically domestic banks in such countries only lend on a short-term basis;
- Technology transfer: project finance provides a way of producing market-based investment in infrastructure for which the local economy may have neither the resources nor the skills.

For project finance to take hold, there needs to be substantial sources of funding available either within the country or foreign capital that is able to freely enter the market in question. To recap from chapter 4, these sources are the following:

1. *Commercial loans*: from commercial banks and DFIs
2. *Equity*: usually from private investors
3. *Subordinated loans*: loans repaid with priority over equity but subordinated to commercial loans
4. *Supplier's credit*: loans provided by project equipment suppliers
5. *Export Credit Agency (ECA)*: facilities loans, guarantees, or insurance

Therefore, a substantial depth in availability of each of the above sources of funding is needed in developing markets and developers, especially independent ones without multinational parent company balance sheets to back them up, will need to assess their target market for this depth of availability.

CHAPTER 7

Case Study: Riga, Latvia

Latvia is a very interesting location for our case study as a country that imports 100 percent of its fossil fuels from Russia. Latvia gained its independence from the Soviet Union in 1991 and joined the European Union (EU) in 2004. Latvia's electricity generation mix is made up of hydropower, fossil fuels, biomass (including peat resources), waste, and wind.

With this background, we can turn to our case study. It involves a biomass plant that was developed in response to the need to provide low-carbon heat. In the context of government incentives of feed-in tariffs (FiT), which we have seen extensively before, the developers were able to successfully develop and fund the project.

What I would like the reader to take note of especially is the application of the principles that we have covered in this book in a real-life situation. The case study covers the regulatory framework and how the developer had to navigate it. It covers the choice of technology and contractor. We see the experience of permitting and how that can affect the viability of the project. We see how the developer overcomes the challenge of finding the right partners, both on the contractor side and crucially with respect to co-investors. Last but not least, the case study highlights the challenges around raising bank financing which required no little amount of persistence from the developer.

Don't invent the bicycle, just copy/paste good working solutions
—Dmitrijs Artusins

Project Summary: Overview of Project Motivation

- The motivation behind the project was the production of green energy with the aim to sell thermal energy to Riga Municipality. The company wanted to compete with the local utility and earn FiTs.

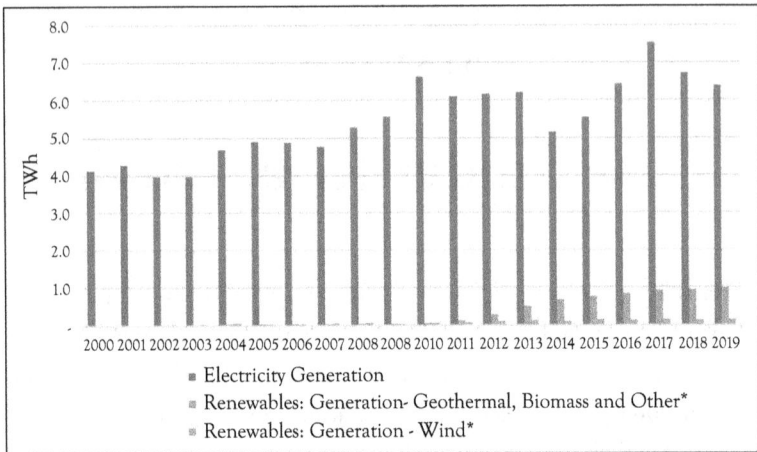

Figure 7.1 Latvia electricity generation

Source: bp Statistical Review 2020.

*Based on gross generation and not accounting for cross-border electricity supply. From Figure 7.1, we can see that renewables make up a growing but modest share of the generation base. With access to plentiful supplies of Russian gas, growth in renewable technologies, such as biomass and wind, did not take off until 2012.

- o Initially the FiT was linked to gas prices but now prices are fixed (144.19 rubles per MWh). The installed capacity is 4 MW and the PPA provides 32,000MWh p.a. to the Municipality equating to installed capacity of 4 MW × 8,000 hours.
- o The project is connected to the municipal thermal network that serves Riga, a city with a population of close to one million.
- o The developer believes that 2.5 percent of the city's thermal demand can be met by green energy.

Technology

- Characteristics
  - o *Biomass Combined Heat and Power (CHP)*—2,000 components/steam boiler and steam turbine. The presence of a fuel gas condenser makes the system very efficient.
  - o *Fuel input*—Wood chips are used to produce steam and the condenser cools (using municipal water) the turbine and fuel gas.

Rationale Behind the Technology

What factors (e.g., around resource, cost, availability, and maintenance) led to the choices that the developer made in bringing this project to completion?

Input fuel:

1. Biomass—53 percent of Latvia is covered in forest, making it the most sustainable resource in the area. There is a law in Latvia that requires the replanting or replacement of the same amount of biomass that has been harvested. Forests are also regularly cleared of debris and this can be used as an additional biomass resource.
2. Solar—not a consideration as the region has half the irradiation intensity of Spain.
3. Hydro—lots of hydro schemes already in the country with no new sites available.
4. Wind—no FiT available for wind projects.
5. Waste treatment—seen as not as sustainable as biomass—it is not sustainable to grow crops and use them to produce energy; land can be used more efficiently for other purposes.

Technology provider: Available product/service support from the manufacturer. The technology provider (Dutch company, Host Bio-energy Installations) already had offices in Riga and a local team. Their track record included four biomass and three biogas projects in Latvia.

The developers were therefore fully convinced that they could reliably build and maintain the plant. The Project Company enjoys ongoing service support (O&M contractor) from the company that built the plant (EPC contractor) and its engineers, who themselves deal with all the subcontractors. The developer had a strong requirement for a contractor who could provide a full service, of which there were only three in the country. Furthermore, one of the prerequisites from the lending bank was that a local company should provide the service for the project if the bank were to finance it.

Core Principles

- Development process
  - Procurement

1. Partnership structure—two individuals (Sponsors) with the initial sum of investment to get the project off the ground.
2. Choice of technology after an in-depth study of available options.
3. After the right technology and contractor was chosen, preliminary technical information was developed.
4. Design and basic engineering were carried out (pre-FEED) and a building permit was acquired.
5. In the interim, the developers searched for potential investors and were open to a different variety of options for example, to build and sell right away, sell later, and so on.
6. The developer partnered with investors that already had similar experience and these new partners agreed to become the operators of the plant. This made good sense as the new investors already had experience from previous (four in total) successful projects. Together, all the partners agreed to sell the plant after the first year of operations.
7. After the building permit was approved within a short space of time, the bank credit was approved, and the developer was able to make a down payment for the equipment.
8. The EPC Contractor provided the technology. A separate contract with a construction company provided for the civil works and another for connection to the grid. The latter contract was carried out by the government-owned utility that is responsible for operating the electricity grid. Finally, a fourth contract was required to provide for the connection to the thermal grid.

- Legal and Regulatory
  1. The project was the first private biomass project connected to the municipal heat network. The grid owner had to come up with new methods and techniques (legal and regulatory) for a connection of privately owned plant to the municipal network. The project therefore paved the way and other developers have subsequently sought advice on how to achieve it.
  2. The biggest hurdle for the success of the project was the bank's reluctance to provide funding based on the weekly

heat tender system in Latvia. Heat is sold to the grid in weekly contracts which are awarded to the companies with the lowest price. The Municipality is under obligation to buy heat at the lowest prices. The developers were confident that they would be able to produce heat at a lower price than that of gas but the banks were not. Out of six banks approached, only one was happy to provide the developers with funding.

○ Permits

1. Applied for FiT to the Ministry of Economics, which, in turn, does its own due diligence on the applicants. Once the Ministry was satisfied, it provided the company with a 10-year contract for 32,000 MWh per year. Once a permit is obtained the Project Company has five years to begin operations, otherwise they lose the contract.

○ Feasibility, engineering design

1. Given the previous track record of the new partners (this was their fifth project), for the developers the feasibility work was relatively light touch as they were aware of costs (Capex and Opex), understood the cash flows and already had good in-country experience.

2. The developers wanted a turnkey solution for technology that was already proven to work. Another similar project in the region that had taken on a different technology solution— one that employed exciting and innovative technology—did not manage to reach operations within the five-year time limit and as a result lost their FiT contract. The developers wanted to employ a good running solution: "Let's expand what is already running and not invent something new." It is worth noting here that the developers' goal was not to work on the project for the 10 years but to sell it after one year.

3. The developers chose an engineering team with whom they had worked well previously and had good relations, which made communications very easy. The developers had previously worked on their first two projects with smaller companies but found this approach time-consuming and so they decided, from then on, to work with a larger company.

4. One of the developers (the interviewee) is a thermal engineer and has worked his entire career in the sector, giving him all the technical knowledge needed for the project development and a good ability to oversee the progress of construction and commissioning. He started working at his father's construction company from a young age. Later he worked as a heating systems designer and then built up a small team of five to develop projects from scratch. Each of the team members has a specific set of knowledge and expertise and collectively, they could rely on a large professional network. The developer described himself and his colleagues as a "small team, but very experienced." This is the typical structure of many independent project developers.

- Offtake
  1. FiT for electricity—10-year PPA for 32,000 MWh per year at a fixed price.
  2. Heat—weekly tenders where six plants (three gas and three biomass) participate in the tender process. If there are higher prices for electricity, then the gas price can go down. Biomass was cheaper than the gas and developers were confident that they could produce heat at a price lower than that of gas. The average consumption in Riga is 450 MW per hour during the heating season while the average peak is 1,000 MW per hour and lowest in summer is 80 MW per hour.

- Fuel Supply
  1. Woodchips—open tender. There are many companies, the supply chains are highly developed, and so the developers were not concerned with this piece of the puzzle. Latvia is an exporter of woodchips to neighboring Finland and Sweden. In Riga, demand is met by the supply when needed and there is no over production of woodchips. Latvia is third in Europe for production of wood pellets.

- Financing arrangements
  1. Local bank—out of six banks approached, five refused because of risk of not selling due to the weekly tender system for thermal heat. As stated earlier, the developers were

confident of their project's ability to produce heat at a lower price than gas, but the banks needed more convincing. Out of six banks that they applied to, only one agreed to provide them with funding.

2. The project was selected among industry circles as the best biomass project in Latvia on the criteria of technology and financial viability.

Social, Economic, Technological, and Regulatory Drivers and Barriers in the Project Development

- Main drivers in carrying out the project
  - FiT—financial driver
  - Motivation—no other biomass plant was connected to heating network with biomass/gas price
  - In emerging renewable energy markets, the players are fewer and smaller, which allows for competition.
  - According to the developer, the lead-time for developing a project is less than in an already developed market as you work mostly with companies that you know well.
  - The developer also felt that the tender process is easier in an emerging market.
- Main Barriers
  - Bank financing
  - Weekly heat contract

Drivers and Barriers to Developing a Project in an Emerging/ Frontier Market

- Cost, profitability, and competitiveness of renewable energy options in those markets
  - Biomass/wood pellet is less expensive than gas, while all the other renewable energy sources/technologies need subsidies in order to be competitive in Latvia's energy market.
  - In Latvia, there were many grants from the EU in order to subsidize the transition from gas to biomass, which led to a

behavioral change in the population and wider adoption of the technology. Now around 70 percent of thermal energy in Latvia is delivered by biomass.

- Energy sector structure
  - Two companies own the electricity grid and there is an open market for trading, where 20+ companies act as traders.
  - The gas sector is also an open market for trading
  - Municipal—each city has its own network where the regulator monitors the market. If a project/plant wants to enter the market, they have to provide benefits for end-users, in terms of lower tariffs. Each municipal company can sign an independent provider if they can demonstrate that there will be benefits to the end-users. Interestingly, the fact that the project will provide green electricity is not considered as a benefit to the end-user in and of itself; cost and security of supply is key.
- Financial risks for renewable energy
  - The developer sees the biggest risk in renewable energy project development as a regulatory one, due to the absence of FiT for new projects. There is no specific legislation for renewable energy, which means that the government can change regulations depending on how cabinet changes and what policies are in place. At any point, the cabinet regulations can change formula and prices, which contributes to the uncertainty of developing and financing renewable energy projects.

Sustainable Return on Investment (SROI)

- SROI as part of the development plan
  - SROI was not considered by the developers
  - Associated SROI benefits from the projects
    1. Lower price for the consumers
    2. Natural gas replaced with local biomass so local regeneration and local people are part of the supply chain
    3. Local contracts for the development

- Did the project developers consider the wider social, economic, and environmental impact? If so, what are results? If not, should it be part of future development projects and why?
  - Unfortunately, nobody is thinking about SROI, be they regulators or developers. In the opinion of the developer, SROI definitely should feature prominently in the development of projects and possibly needs to be subsidized by the government.

Conditions for the Development Approach to Be Transferred and Adopted in Other Emerging and Frontier Markets

- What are the main requirements/preconditions for transferring the project and applying it elsewhere?
  - Technically, it can be fully replicated. It has already been transferred and replicated in two projects in Croatia by the same project team from Latvia.
  - Economically, it very much depends on circumstances (FiT, heat incentives, etc). In addition, it very much depends on the availability of resources and price of the resources.
  - Another variable is the knowledge and expertise of the team developing the project.
- **Project results**
  - Benefits
    1. All parties to the project development and operations were satisfied and there was an economic gain for all parties.
    2. The company that is now operating the plant is content with the working hours of the plant and return on investment.
    3. Developers have capital with which to develop further projects.
    4. The Municipality has one more producer on the network providing further options and lowering the price for consumers.
    5. For the local economy, the usage of biomass through local supply chains rather than exporting it to other countries, cutting costs for both sides.

- Lessons learned
    1. Developers should research and double, even triple check, all the technical aspects of a project beforehand, so that no delays are caused in the next step of the development.
    2. The developer also advised direct communication with all parties involved. This approach of talking to all parties relevant to the development personally and directly is done with the objective of understanding their attitude to your project. For example, the developer advises having a meeting with the municipal company at the very beginning of project conception to make a judgment on the likelihood of obtaining a contract once the latter parts of the project puzzle are in place.

CHAPTER 8

Raising Money and Attracting the Right Investor

In this book, we repeatedly refer to the developer. The question is who stands behind the developer? The sponsors are often investors in both the Project Company and the developer, but sometimes the developer is independent and seeking funding for the Project Company alone. This chapter will be of particular use to smaller developers who do not have a parent company's large balance sheet sitting behind them. The likes of Engie, ENEL, Acciona et al. are corporate behemoths within which sit developer teams in business units that operate the Project Companies as subsidiaries or joint ventures.

As an independent developer, it will often seem as if you have a constant requirement for funding. The costs involved with developing an energy project are constant and, at times, unpredictable. While the need for money can seem overwhelming, I can recommend an approach to raising finance and attracting the right kind of investor.

Before You Start Negotiations

The following questions should be asked:

1. At what stage of the project lifecycle are you currently?
2. How much ownership are you, as a developer, willing to give?
3. How much time, money, and effort do you need to reach the project launch?

1. At what stage of the project lifecycle are you currently?

Referring to Chapter 3 on structural aspects of a project and the Project Lifecycle you will be familiar with the three main phases of a project:

1. *Development*: Feasibility studies, permits, environmental and social impact assessment, basic and detailed front-end engineering and design
2. *Implementation*: Construction and commissioning
3. *Operations*: Generation of value and servicing of debts

From an investor's perspective, the stage of your project will determine its risk profile and, by extension, the project's valuation. All things being equal, the further along you are in the project lifecycle, the less risk perceived by investors. Different risk profiles will attract certain kinds of investors. Put simply, the more risk perceived by an investor or bank, the higher the return they will demand.

Once you are at the stage where all contractual agreements are secured and the project is ready for financial close, the more likely that low risk, steady return investors such as private equity and infrastructure and pension funds will be attracted to invest in your project.

On the flip side, should you be at an earlier phase, the more likely that a venture capital-type or specialist investor, with a deep knowledge of the kind of project that you are developing, will be attracted to invest. While most people would typically look toward the financial services sector for an investor, I would encourage developers to look at finding investment support from the project's foundation stakeholders.

2. How much ownership are you, as a developer, willing to give?

Most developers let personal attachment to their project get in the way of any talk about raising money. You need to be as dispassionate and rational as possible. I have seen so many negotiations run aground because of a developer's unrealistic expectations as to how much he or she is willing to give up in return for investment.

The fact of the matter is, you need money and someone else can provide it under certain terms. At the earlier stages of the project lifecycle, you should base your valuation not on what the model says the project will eventually generate but on how much time, effort, and money you have put into the project to date. Time, money, and effort are relatively easy to record and can be a useful basis for framing your own account of how much you have put into the project and how much more is required to achieve the project's realization.

3. How much time, money, and effort do you need to reach the project launch?

The answer to this question will be of use to you when calculating how much of these three factors you have, as a developer, put into the project to date and what you have achieved as a result. From an investor's point of view, they will evaluate closely what has been achieved and use this to evaluate how much time, effort, and money they will need to put in order to realize their own return on investment. Having a realistic idea, from your side, of how much of these three factors are still needed will greatly help you in any negotiations.

Engaging Investors

Now that you have asked, and hopefully answered, the three questions posed earlier; you will need to begin the process of engaging potential investors. My recommendation is to start as close to home as possible. Foundation stakeholders will have a more intimate knowledge of your project than most people will and so should need less time to get up to speed with the finer points of risk and valuation. A line of approach for each is suggested below.

Equipment suppliers: Most equipment suppliers are manufacturers or resellers who are only interested in generating sales. For them to invest in your project would require you, as a developer, to demonstrate the reward to them of taking on additional risk. Why would they do so? As the developer, it is your task to sell the benefits of the project to them, which could include:

- High-profile entry into a new market
- Pilot project to test a new product
- Significant financial benefit above and beyond that from straightforward sales

Now you will have noticed that the second benefit offers significant risk to you—being a guinea pig for new technology is not an ideal scenario and you will have to make a judgment based on your requirements at the time. Should the project prove to be a success, the last benefit will mean that you, as project owner, would have sacrificed a significant upside of the project—that of financial gain.

The aforementioned benefits cover both strategic and financial interests of the equipment supplier. It is up to you as the developer to identify and research the best-suited equipment supplier for your project based on your needs. This process naturally involves some compromise—you may not end up with the biggest or the "best" supplier in the market, however, you will have achieved your goal of obtaining funding and moved closer to your objective of delivering your own energy project.

Offtakers: In my experience, raising money from an Offtaker which is a private entity, will be easier than doing so from a government entity. Government entities' interests tend to span wider than those of any other stakeholder. When approaching and persuading your Offtaker to participate, let alone invest, in your project you will need to have answered several questions:

1. Is the project value for money? Here you will have to demonstrate that the cost of the energy service compares relatively favorably with that of alternatives. This is a challenging task mainly because of the time and effort that will be required to perform the necessary research into the cost of alternative energy sources.

2. Is it affordable? There is no sense in approaching a government Offtaker for investment if you know that they cannot afford to invest. This is where your research into international sources of funding, provided by the likes of the International Finance Corporation, can be of great use to developers operating in emerging markets.

3. Can it be achieved? The answer to this question lies in your ability to demonstrate your own capabilities as a developer of delivering the project to expectations.

4. Is it necessary? Energy is a necessity for any economy and the provision of low carbon and sustainable energy in a post-COVID-19, net zero carbon context is even more so. The challenge here is that

the government in question will be weighing up your project with its other priorities for example, food security, poverty, natural disasters, and so on.

Your "pitch" will need to demonstrate at several levels that the project will be of an overall benefit to the government Offtaker's interest. By contrast, convincing a private entity to invest in the project will require you to demonstrate that their commercial, strategic, and financial interests are met.

EPC Contractor: These contractors operate in a highly competitive space and are constantly on the lookout for new projects in which to participate. That being the case, the opportunity to participate free of any tendering or competition is usually an attractive one and should be an option that you explore when seeking investment. An EPC contractor who also invests in the project will be as committed as you are to ensuring its success. You should therefore approach EPC contractors as potential partners that can be of benefit to you, the developer, in terms of completing the project.

Until your project is within striking distance of achieving financial close, I would not advise you to consider investment from professional investors. Professional investors that is, private equity funds, banks and so on require a very different approach when raising money. The cornerstone of discussions with them will be your project's financial model and the term sheet you should have obtained from the Lead Arranger.

This will need to be developed to an advanced stage and with as many of the assumptions verified independently. Many developers, given their nature and educational background, opt to work on the financial model themselves. My advice would be to not do so—engage a specialist who is impartial and can develop the model to a higher degree of detail than you can. As we saw in the chapter on financial aspects of the core principles, there will be several versions of the financial model by the time financial close is reached. Hiring a financial advisor or even letting the Lead Arranger take on this role makes good business sense. Let me assure you, a professional investor's financial analysts will dig into the model to a depth and level of detail that most nonspecialists do not have the time or ability to achieve. You are therefore better off focusing on other areas that will benefit more from your particular skill-set as a developer.

Next Steps

Any advancement in investment-related discussions will usually involve a term sheet being exchanged. This is simply a document that lists the mains terms under which two parties agree to progress discussions or negotiations toward a formal contract. A term sheet typically contains the clauses shown in Table 8.1.

Table 8.1 Contents of a typical term sheet

Background and legal preamble	This will contain what the purpose of the term sheet document is from a legal perspective. It is important to state that the term sheet is an initial agreement, which will set the parameters for further discussions, and a more formal agreement later. It will be helpful to recount the history of discussions between the parties and what the respective expectations of both parties are from having these discussions.
Glossary	Most legal agreements contain a section where both technical terms and acronyms, both those that are general and those specific to the term sheet, are defined.
Definition of the parties	It is stated here who are the legal entities involved.
Description of the project	This will contain detail on the project that the developer has been working on.
Description of the transaction	In this case, the transaction would be either a sale of equity in the project to an investor, or a loan to the project by a bank.
Duration	The length of time for which the term sheet is valid.
Confidentiality	The term sheet should be confidential between the parties with no information shared to other parties without the written consent of the disclosing party. It is usual to widen the scope of confidentiality to include foundation stakeholders who may wish there to be transparency over any discussions between the developer and funding partners.
Exclusivity	An investor will usually place a restriction on the developer discussing with other potential investors. This is because some time and effort will need to be spent in order to turn a potential deal into a closed one.
Due diligence	This will cover specific areas that the investor/bank will want time to study: commercial, financial, legal, technical, tax, and so on. In short, the investor will want to verify all of the information that has been provided by the developer.
Applicable law	An oft-overlooked detail. Most parties will stipulate the jurisdiction with which they are most familiar. Government entities rarely sign agreements under a foreign country's jurisdiction. For many parts of the world, English law offers a convenient compromise.

The list in Table 8.1 is not exhaustive and term sheets can contain many more clauses that will reflect the investor or bank's requirements.

If you are fortunate enough to have reached the point where you are considering a term sheet from an investor, the main point to consider is that the time and effort required passing due diligence will be considerable. During this phase, the investor will go through every aspect of the project with a fine-toothed comb. The parallels with this process and that of the due diligence with the Lead Arranger should not be lost on the reader. Indeed, some efficiencies can be gained by integrating the two processes as much as possible to save time. The following list is designed to give you an idea of the areas that will be examined:

Commercial: All contractual arrangements in your project will be scrutinized. Most developers tend to focus all their time on the offtake agreement, which, while crucial, is not the only commercial arrangement that can jeopardize the bankability of a project. Engineering, Procurement and Construction (EPC) contracts are often overlooked by developers who end up taking the first contract offered to them. An EPC contract should primarily offer a high degree of certainty on the Capex and the start date of the operations and contain provision to mitigate any associated risks.

Financial: All the financial implications associated with your project will be tested. From the investor or bank's point of view, their main concern here is on the affordability of the project to sustain the repayment of their investment under adverse conditions.

Legal: The legal validity of ownership and rights pertaining to the project. The investor will examine all permits, land documents, lease agreements, history of ownership, regulations, and evaluate what adverse risks or material impact these could have on the valuation of the project.

Technical: Technical due diligence will revolve around the choice of technology. Is the equipment expected to perform to the required standard over the course of the project's life span? Questions such as whether equipment will need replacing, and what provision has been made for replacement and maintenance, will be raised. Once again, the main concern here is whether the technology poses a risk to the investor of recouping their investment.

Once due diligence has been completed final negotiations around valuation may take place. At this point the developer may find that their earlier expectations around valuation may be challenged, while I would not encourage a developer to "give up the farm," I would stress that you are at the point where the investor or bank have something that you need—money, and that this money is tantalizingly close. You should therefore be pragmatic and keep your eyes on the objective.

Post Financial Close, the developer's focus should be entirely on overseeing the construction of the project and the subsequent operations. Construction projects, by nature, are highly complex and typically take longer and cost more than originally envisaged. I would advise the developer not to take on the role of project manager of the construction; this considerable task should be left to the EPC contractor who should report on the progress of construction to a steering board on which the main stakeholders, including the developer, should sit. The governance around the Steering Board should follow guidelines set by project management standards of the likes of Prince2 or the Association of Project Management.

CHAPTER 9

Measuring Social and Environmental Impact (Sustainable Return)

Recently it has become increasingly difficult to secure investment for your project without a clear idea of what value in terms of sustainability your project brings. In this chapter we shall look at the definition of Sustainable Return on Investment (SROI), review the United Nations' Sustainable Development Goals, build up a framework and methodology for measuring and reporting the SROI, and look at an alternative methodology.

From working through this chapter, you should increasingly see the interconnectivity between your sustainable project and the United Nation's (UN's) 17 Sustainable Development Goals (SDGs). As we have discussed earlier, these goals have been set in order to face the challenges faced by humanity. This chapter will encourage you to integrate your project with these SDGs to maximize the overall impact of your project, which will in turn mean that the project attracts the right stakeholders.

Taking the development of a project from the perspective of SROI, you should look at the maximization of two metrics—Financial Return on Investment and Sustainable Return on Investment. In that context, these two are inextricably linked. Nevertheless, we shall also briefly go over an alternative methodology, the Total Cost Assessment (TCA), which is an approach that arrives at the same result of a comprehensive, "triple bottom line" project valuation.

Finally, I intend for you to, above all, appreciate from this chapter how energy underpins all human activity on the planet and that your efforts as a sustainable energy developer will be crucial to safeguarding the future of humanity on this planet.

Assessing SROI

The topic of sustainability is gaining in urgency as humanity becomes increasingly aware of the threats it faces. Our environment and natural habitat, thanks to the negative effects of climate change and greenhouse gas emissions, are becoming increasingly fragile and this, in turn, poses far-reaching problems to human beings and society at large. In short, humanity is facing an existential threat and your actions in maximizing the sustainability of your project will contribute to mitigating that threat.

We return to our earlier definition of sustainability; this is the meeting point where economic, social, and environmental benefits all come together as shown in Figure 9.1.

Sustainability, when delivering an energy project, means that the interests of society as a whole are met, not just those of a few stakeholders. There are countless examples from the oil and gas, chemicals, pharmaceutical, and industrial processing industries of environmental and health-related disasters. For you as a sustainable energy developer, it means that you are committed to provide energy without causing environmental damage or causing other negative externalities on society. Calculating the SROI will help you communicate the full value of your project by reporting not just the direct cash benefits but also the indirect and noncash effects that your project will have and present these as a monetary value. This the first step in defining SROI—it seeks to account for a project's

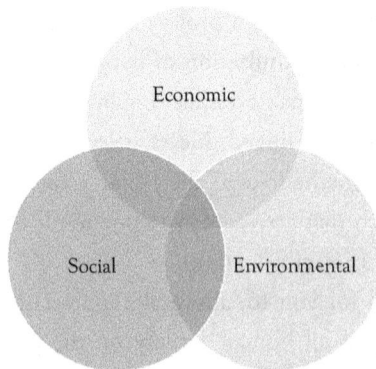

Figure 9.1 The interaction of economic, social, and environmental benefits

triple bottom line. This means that we can estimate the monetary value of a project by accounting for its environmental, social and economic impacts. Benefits that can be generated from a positive triple bottom line could be a reduction in greenhouse gas emissions, reduced air pollution, amount of water conserved, and so on. All of these would, I hope, be the benefits of the kinds of projects dealt with in this book.

You will recall the UN's published 17 interconnected SDGs to help act as a blueprint to meet the challenge that humanity faces and that SDG 7, which tackles Affordable and Clean Energy, is our focus in this book.

By nature, however, energy touches pretty much every area of human activity; this means that in all likelihood your sustainable project will be interconnected with many of the other SDGs:

1. No Poverty
2. Zero Hunger
3. Good Health and Well-Being
4. Quality Education
5. Gender Equality
6. Clean Water and Sanitation
7. *Affordable and Clean Energy*
8. Decent Work and Economic Growth
9. Industry, Innovation, and Infrastructure
10. Reduced Inequalities
11. Sustainable Cities and Communities
12. Responsible Consumption and Production
13. Climate Action
14. Life Below Water
15. Life on Land
16. Peace, Justice, and Strong Institutions
17. Partnerships for the Goals

Why is Goal 7 important? All sectors of economic activity are supported by energy—businesses, agriculture, medicine, manufacturing, and high technology all use vast amounts of energy. In Sub-Saharan Africa alone, according to International Energy Agency (IEA) figures for 2018, around 600 million people lack access to electricity. More attention is needed to increase the use of renewable energy, improve energy efficiency and improve the access to safe cooking fuels and technologies for three billion people globally.

Our centuries-old dependence on fossil fuels have produced huge amounts of greenhouse gases, which cause climate change and harm the environment and people's health. In a world where global consumption of electricity is expected to increase, a sustainable supply of electricity for the future will be needed to prevent poorer countries from being left behind.

At a time when we have seen the world paralyzed by the COVID-19 pandemic, the lack of access to energy may undermine future efforts to fight diseases and pandemics. Goal 7 has the following targets:

7.1 *By 2030, ensure universal access to affordable, reliable and modern energy services*

7.2 *By 2030, increase substantially the share of renewable energy in the global energy mix*

7.3 *By 2030, double the global rate of improvement in energy efficiency*

7.A *By 2030, enhance international cooperation to facilitate access to clean energy research and technology, including renewable energy, energy efficiency and advanced and cleaner fossil-fuel technology, and promote investment in energy infrastructure and clean energy technology*

7.B *By 2030, expand infrastructure and upgrade technology for supplying modern and sustainable energy services for all in developing countries, in particular least developed countries, small island developing States, and land-locked developing countries, in accordance with their respective programmes of support.*[1]

One can make a strong argument for placing Goal 7 as one of the most important, as access to energy boosts economic and social activity that can deliver lasting change. Goal 7 focuses on improving the access to electricity in poorer countries, increasing both energy efficiency and the share of renewable energy in electricity sector.

It will be a strong motivator and helpful for you as an energy developer to be mindful and aware of how your energy project promotes or benefits the other 16 SDGs previously mentioned. It will therefore be of

---

[1] https://sdgs.un.org/goals/goal7

use, when building your SROI framework, to identify how many of the aforementioned SDGs directly or indirectly relate to your project and then measure the project's overall benefit to each SDG.

Having a project with a high SROI means that you both identify and measure the societal, environmental, and economic benefits of your project to all stakeholders including investors. By measuring and reporting the sustainable return throughout the project lifecycle, you will build up a strong ability to view your project through the lens of these interconnected elements and hence be in a strong position to sell your project to the relevant stakeholders. Indeed, under every possible SDG affected, your project may have stakeholders who will need to be involved in the project at some level.

With this in mind, let us now turn to the methodology for identifying and quantifying your SROI.

The standard seven-principle model for the measurement of sustainable return is as follows:

1. Stakeholders: involving everyone who is changed by your project. Involving them in planning what gets measured and how.
2. Understand what changes: develop a story of change and gather evidence of both positive and negative change.
3. Value the things that matter: rate the importance of different outcomes by valuing the economic, social, and environmental benefits and costs of your project.
4. Only include what is material: report on what is relevant and significant.
5. Do not overclaim: compare your results with what would have happened anyway.
6. Be transparent: clearly explain all assumptions and evidence.
7. Verify the results: make use of others to check your results.

With the above principles in mind, we can now outline the steps for undertaking an SROI:

A. Defining the boundaries (Objective and Scope): A specific geographic area covering your project will need to be chosen over a time span matching that of the life span of the project. At this stage, you should have mapped out all the economic, social, and environmental variables of your project and classed them into either costs or benefits. Once the initial mapping is completed, you assign monetary values to each of the variables (see step E below). If needed, you may have to use probability distributions to determine a realistic monetary value for the variable.

B. Identification and Selection of Key Stakeholders: Identify all relevant actors who are affected by or who influence the project (positively or negatively). You should use whatever means are effective to bring these stakeholders on board with the project.

C. Develop the Business Plan: Representatives of all stakeholders take part in the creation of the business plan. At this point, you should refer to the 17 SDGs and identify which of these will be impacted by your project. You should work with the relevant stakeholders to tell the story of how they were involved in the project and their perception of how their lives were changed or will change.

D. What goes in (identify inputs for each outcome) and what comes out (results). For each intended outcome, there are many different investments and costs linked to the realization of the outcome.

E. Valuation is the process of developing indicators that turn the articulated costs and benefits into a monetary value. By nature, some benefits and costs are easier to value than others are for example, electricity costs, greenhouse emissions and so on. You may need to employ different tools to tackle different indicators such as opportunity cost, value ranking, probability distribution and so on.

F. Calculation of the SROI ratio: By calculating the SROI ratio you are making a comparison between the inputs (investments) on the one hand and the economic, social, and environmental benefits (outcomes) on the other. It goes without saying that solid research data enhances the credibility of the ratio derived.

G. Narratives are seen as the qualitative accounts that complement the quantitative (the SROI ratio). They provide the context around the ratio and provide reflection on what cannot be captured within the ratio.

H. Verification is done through the analyses either by triangulation or by other means. Verifying the narratives as well as the quantitative data from different stakeholder perspectives is important as it builds and maintains on the trust and collective ownership of the project.

From Theory to Practice

The previous steps are all you need to undertake in order to obtain the SROI. Let's look at simple case: for a typical energy project you will have a set of data inputs that will cover the following:

1. Energy
2. Emissions
3. Site development
4. Community values
5. Corporate responsibility
6. Waste, water, and other utilities

Once you have the inputs, you go through the process described previously to arrive at the Costs and Benefits Outputs. For a typical renewable energy project, these outputs should include the following:

1. Greenhouse gas savings
2. Energy cost savings
3. Air pollution savings

Assigning a monetary value to the above is not always straightforward but can be determined by drawing on evidence, where possible. For example, some greenhouse gases are traded, such as CO_2 and so a monetary value on the tons of CO_2 saved by your project can be determined. By contrast, energy cost savings are relatively straightforward to calculate, as you should know what is the cost of the electricity you are displacing. Quantifying the savings incurred from reductions in air pollution will require you to collaborate closely with stakeholders such as local environmental or public health agencies. This process of assessment is demonstrated in Figure 9.2.

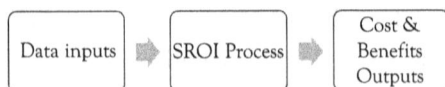

Figure 9.2 Steps to arrive at Costs and Benefits output of a typical energy project

Table 9.1 Projecting and discounting the monetary value of your project's costs and benefits outputs

	Year 1	Year 2	Year 3	Year 4	Year 5
Benefits Energy costs savings GHG Savings Air pollution savings Water savings Green jobs creation	$100,000	$75,000	$50,000	$50,000	$50,000
Discounted values	$$$	$$$	$$$	$$$	$$$
Present value	$$$				

Once you have assigned monetary values to your benefits then you will have to project and discount them as you would your project's cash flows as per Table 9.1.

The net present value (NPV) of your SROI would simply be the difference between the present value of all benefits and the present value of all costs.

In cases where you cannot arrive at a monetary value of the benefits, it still pays to present these in a simple format for example, number of green jobs created, tons of NOX emissions saved and so on.

The SROI ratio is simply the value obtained after dividing the discounted value of the benefits by the total investment:

SROI ratio = Present Value/Total investment

You will seek to generate a positive SROI—if the ratio is 3:1 that means that for every dollar invested your project will generate sustainability value worth three dollars. From the above, it should be clear that the success of your calculation of SROI depends heavily on two factors: accurate data and well-coordinated facilitation of the multiple stakeholders in the project.

An Alternative Approach

An alternative means of arriving at the same result is that of Total Cost Assessment (TCA). This methodology was created by chemical manufacturers and published through the *Journal of the American Institute of Chemical Engineers*. This methodology was intended to take health and environmental costs, which at times can be very unpredictable, into consideration in order to aid decision making around investments.

As in the SROI methodology, you begin by listing all the costs and benefits with the difference being that you categorize these costs and benefits as either internal (borne by the company) or external (borne by society at large). Economists call the latter "externalities" and far too many projects in the past have caused such external costs with no mitigation cost borne by the project sponsor.

In addition to direct and indirect costs and benefits, TCA takes into account contingent liabilities and internal and external intangibles. Bringing all of these together you can build up the list below:

1. *Direct costs*: These will be one-off costs such as Capex and recurring costs such as Opex and maintenance costs.
2. *Indirect costs*: Project development costs including reporting and feasibility studies. The rule of thumb here is to place costs that are not directly attributable to the production of the energy that your project sells, into this category.
3. *Future and contingent liability costs*: Any potential liabilities incurred by accidents or noncompliance. You should quantify any costs that can arise from things going wrong during construction and operations. You will need to rely on third parties and information from similar projects to help in defining these costs.
4. *Intangible internal costs*: Community relations costs, employee, and staff welfare. These can be difficult to measure from the outset and the true nature of their scale may only be known after a sustained period of operations.
5. *Intangible external costs*: Negative effects on environment, natural habitat, and public health. Again, these can be hard to measure so you will need to rely on some sort of probabilistic analysis involving historical data.

From this we can see that the TCA methodology, like SROI, looks at all three main aspects of sustainability (environmental, social, and economic) but comes at it from a different aspect of looking exclusively at costs and at minimizing these. The logic of this being that, by minimizing the environmental, economic, and social costs of a project, we are best placed to maximize the project's benefits to society as a whole. Where TCA falls short of SROI is that SROI considers the potential benefits of all variables as well as the costs. Further details on the TCA methodology can be found in the list of references at the end of this book.

Conclusion

The focus of this book, aside from arming the reader with a grasp of the fundamentals required to develop projects, has been on the energy transition and project development in developing countries. The outlook for renewable power generation projects in developing countries has never looked brighter. The year 2019 marked a record-breaking year for signature of PPAs by the private sector[1] and with governments around the world increasing their climate ambitions, the addition of more renewable generation capacity should accelerate in those countries that are further behind the curve. According to REN21, renewable energy capacity investment in developing countries (outside of China and India) totaled $59.5 billion.

In late 2020 we know that over 100 developing countries now have targets and or policies in place to encourage investment in renewable electricity. Key to setting the right environment is government policy in the jurisdiction in question. Developers need to have incentives whether they be feed-in tariffs, tax incentives, reductions in subsidies for fossil fuels, or simply targets for renewable energy generation. As we have seen in the preceding pages and in particular those covering our case study, gaps in policy can offer hurdles to the developer but by no means do they preclude the successful completion of projects.

One policy incentive that is worth looking out for, which developing countries are expected to take up, is that around carbon pricing; taxes on carbon emissions, emissions trading systems and carbon credits can all indirectly incentivize the development of renewable energy generation. They do this by increasing the cost of burning fossil fuels and thereby reduce environmental pollution and degradation.

As a developer, you will be confronted by policymakers who get it right and those who do not. Being acutely aware, as early as possible, of what mixture of policies and targets are required for your project will

---

[1] *Renewables 2020 Global Status report* – Ren21.

make the difference between success and failure. Take our Latvia case study for example, the developers considered and then eliminated several different types of technologies before landing on the biomass option. The presence of a FiT for biomass but not for other technologies was a deciding factor.

The projects highlighted in this book covered a wide range of sizes, from the 15 MW solar plant in West Africa to the 850 MW+ projects that took place in Morocco and elsewhere. What should be clear is that there is space for all sizes of projects in developing countries, where so-called decentralized energy projects (those projects that produce energy off the main grid) in particular, will see a surge in popularity. Smaller independent developers will take an interest in projects that they can handle, while the larger multinationals will look for the competitive tenders and capacity auctions to generate the kinds of returns that they need.

We have looked at renewable technologies (biomass, solar PV, onshore and offshore wind among them) and noted which ones are better suited to certain markets. We saw how CSP is costly compared to other technologies but that unlike solar PV, thanks to thermal energy storage, CSP can offer round-the-clock energy supply. Like other technologies that have gone through similar development cycles, the costs will come down as the CSP industry becomes more geographically diverse.

We looked at the challenges around raising finance, in the form of loans from the bank and then from other sources like equity investors. Again, our case study throws up an important lesson. With respect to the equity investor, bringing on board a partner who already has expertise in the sector will take you a very long way toward reaching your goal. In the case of the commercial loans, persistence is the key to success. The developers were convinced of their project's ability to produce heat cheaper than gas and so stuck with their efforts, which in the end proved successful.

Finally, measuring the Sustainable Return on Investment will become a standard element of the project development process. In the wider economic context, we have seen large companies become more transparent in reporting how their operations stack up against Environmental, Social, and Governance (ESG) criteria. Calculating the SROI is simply a project-level version of the ESG framework and in time we will see investors apply this more and more on their portfolios. In addition to applying the thinking around SROI to your project, it will be of great benefit to promote how your project ties in with the UN's SDGs to lenders, investors and other stakeholders.

I hope that this book has met or even exceeded your expectations. When I first embarked on writing it, I found that there were very few project finance–related publications looking at the subject in a nonacademic and practical manner, from the perspective of the developer. There were even fewer considering exclusively developing countries. It has been a pleasure to share my knowledge of the subject with you and wish you the very best in your project development endeavors.

Glossary of Terms

Arrangement Fee	A fee paid to a mandated bank or group of banks (lead arrangers) for arranging a transaction. It includes fees to be paid to participating banks.
Availability Factor	A measure of how much a power plant is available to produce power, usually expressed as the ratio (a percentage) of a power plant's available hours to the total number of hours in such a period.
Bankable	Capable of being financed.
Balance of Plant (BoP)	Includes all the components of an energy generating resource except the actual generating assets themselves e.g., turbines or solar PV panels; includes transmission assets.
Base Load Plant	A power plant that runs all the time, as opposed to a plant that is used only in times of peak electricity requirements (a peaking plant).
Build–Lease–Transfer (BLT)	The situation when a private owner builds an infrastructure facility, leases it for use, and then transfers it to another entity after a specified period.
Build–Own–Operate (BOO)	The project structure whereby the developer builds the asset in question has full ownership of the asset and maintains the responsibility of operating the asset.

Build–Own–Operate-Transfer (BOOT)	The project structure whereby the developer builds the asset in question, has full ownership of the asset, maintains the responsibility of operating the asset, and then transfers the asset back to the Contracting Authority after a specified period of time (typically somewhere between 25 and 30 years in the transport sector and 15 and 25 years for energy and waste/water).
Build–Operate–Transfer (BOT)	The project structure whereby the developer builds the asset in question, maintains the responsibility of operating the asset, and then transfers the asset back to the Contracting Authority after a specified period of time (typically somewhere between 25 and 30 years in the transport sector and 15 and 25 years for energy and waste/water).
Build–Own–Transfer (BOT)	The situation when a private owner builds, owns, and then transfers an infrastructure facility to another party, often at no cost, after a specified period.
Build–Transfer–Operate (BTO)	The situation when a private owner builds an infrastructure facility, transfers it to another entity, and then operates it on a contractual basis for a specified period.
Capital Expenditure (CapEx)	Long-term expenditures for property, plant, and equipment.
Capacity Factor	Ratio of annual energy production to maximum energy production if the energy-generating asset ran at rated power all year.
Carbon Emissions	Any process that produces CO_2 emissions, usually by burning fossil fuels.

Carbon Offsetting	Reducing emissions or capturing carbon in one sector in order to allow another sector to still produce emissions.
Carbon Neutral	The aim of having no carbon dioxide emissions produced. If any are produced, they are offset by carbon reducing processes.
Cash Waterfall (or Cash Flow Waterfall)	The order of priority for project cash flows as established under the loan and financing documents.
Climate Action100+	Climate Action 100+ is a five-year initiative led by investors to engage systemically important greenhouse gas emitters and other companies across the global economy that have significant opportunities to drive the clean energy transition and achieve the goals of the Paris Agreement. The companies include 100 "systemically important emitters," accounting for two-thirds of annual global industrial emissions, alongside more than 60 others with significant opportunity to drive the clean energy transition.
Climate Emergency	A declaration, usually at national government level, that prioritizes a net zero carbon future. Recent declarations have set this date to 2040 (example).
Cogeneration	The production of energy from the waste heat of industrial processes.
Combined Heat and Power (CHP)	CHP is an energy efficient technology that generates electricity and captures the heat that would otherwise be wasted to provide useful thermal energy that be used for heating, cooling, domestic hot water, and industrial processes.

Completion Guarantee	A guarantee that ensures a project will achieve physical and/or financial completion. A turnkey contractor guarantees physical completion (achievement of certain operating performance). Performance bonds and/ or penalties in the form of liquidated damages normally secure the guarantees. Alternatively, project sponsors sometimes provide lenders with completion guarantees by agreeing to pay the scheduled debt service in the event the Project Company does not or cannot pay.
Commercial lenders	The parties, typically international banks but may also include local banks, who provide financial backing to the project, taking an interest by way of security—often of the asset in question or the project as a whole.
Commercial Operations Date (COD)	The date on which the construction phase of the project is successfully completed (typically determined by some form of independent certification and/or testing regime); the scheduled COD represents a target date for such successful completion with failures to achieve that date having commercial consequences (typically delay liquidated damages and/or termination).
Community engagement	Steps taken to ensure that the project in question can adequately function in the local community. This may be by developing the land in a way that is as compliant as possible with local customs, employing a certain number of local citizens or engaging with local businesses.

Concession Agreement /Power Purchase Agreement (PPA)	The agreement made between a host government and a Project Company or sponsor to permit the construction, development, and operation of a particular project. It outlines the terms on which the project will be undertaken (e.g., BOO, BOOT, BOT). In the energy sector, this is typically the PPA.
Conditions Precedent (CPs)	A set of preconditions that must be satisfied before the borrower can request drawdown or other credit facilities to be made available under a lending agreement.
Consumer Price Index (CPI)	The consumer price index or similar metric that provides for the project parties to account for inflationary effects in the project agreements.
Country Risk	Narrowly defined, this refers to cross-currency and foreign exchange availability risks. More broadly defined, it can also include the political risks of doing business in a given country.
Debt Service	Principal repayments plus interest payable; usually expressed as the annual amount due per calendar or financial year.
Debt Service Coverage Ratio (DSCR)	A quantitative measure used by lenders to determine whether a project has projected net cash flows can support a given amount of debt.
Debt Service Reserve Account (DSRA)	A reserve account set up to ensure the timely payment of principal and interest.
Decarbonization	The process of removing all energy sources that produce carbon emissions from the energy grid.
Discount Rate	The annual percentage rate used to determine the present value of future cash flows.
Drawdown	An actual takedown of money by the borrower under the terms of a loan facility.

Energy Efficiency	The amount of useful energy produced per unit of fuel. The more energy produced or used, the higher the energy efficiency. For example, loft insulation keeps the useful hot air in the home, increasing the energy efficiency of the building.
Energy-Generating Asset	All assets associated with the production of electricity, including generation plants and all related facilities.
Energy Return on Energy Invested (EROI)	This shows the energy that is available to an economy after the energy costs of obtaining that energy are paid. A calculation pioneered by researchers Cutler Cleveland, Charles Hall, Robert Herendeen, and Randall Plant.
Engineering, Procurement, Construction and Installation (EPCI)	A form of contracting arrangement where the contractor is made responsible for all the activities from procurement and construction to commissioning and handover of the project to the principal/owner. Often, referred to as a lump-sum turnkey contract. The contractor delivers via its own and subcontract resources. The word "installation" is often dropped thereby abbreviating this to EPC.
Environmental and Social Impact Assessment (ESIA)	Assessment of the potential impact of the proposed development on the physical, biological, and human environment during construction, operation, and decommissioning.
Equator Principles	Risk management framework, adopted by financial institutions, for determining, assessing, and managing environmental and social risk in projects. It is primarily intended to provide a minimum standard for due diligence to support responsible risk decision making. These can be found at: http://www.equator-principles.com/

Equity	Monies used to finance a deal that is sourced from the existing finances of a company (for example, raised through the issuing of shares in the company), rather than though external debt (for example, from commercial lenders).
Equity return	The amount of a company's net income returned as a percentage of the shareholders' equity.
Export Credit Agency (ECA)	An organization that assists in supporting exports from its country using direct loan and guarantee mechanisms provided by importers.
Expropriation	Where the government takes privately owned property and declares it for public use.
Feed in Tariff (FiT)	A payment made to households or businesses generating their own electricity using methods that do not contribute to the depletions of natural resources, proportional to the amount of power generated.
Final Investment Decision (FID)	The point at which a developer has in place all the consents, agreements, and major contracts required to commence project construction (or these are near execution form) and there is a firm commitment from equity holders and debt funders to provide funding to cover the majority of construction costs.
Finance Documents	The key finance documentation that typically includes a facility agreement with one or more commercial lenders, an intercreditor agreement between the commercial lenders, equity investors, and developer, direct agreement(s) and security documents.

Force majeure	An event, outside the control of the contract-ing parties, that results in one or both of the parties being unable to fulfil their contractual obligations. In common-law jurisdictions, the definition of force majeure is typically a matter of drafting and negotiation whilst in civil law jurisdictions is normally set out in the relevant civil or commercial code.
Free Cash Flow (FCF)	Cash available for capital providers. It is defined as earnings before interest payments adjusted for taxes (EBIAT); plus depreciation, amortization, and other noncash charges; less capital expenditures; less increases in net working capital.
Front End Engineering and Design (FEED)	Front-end engineering and design (FEED) studies address areas of energy system design and develop the concept in advance of pro-curement, contracting, and construction.
Gearing	A measure of leverage such as the ratio of debt to equity or debt to total capitalization.
Gigawatt (GW) and Gigawatt hour (GWh)	Unit of power and unit of energy.
Greenfield	Refers to a project being conceived and exe-cuted where no Project Company, assets, or operations exist. A greenfield site or project location is one where no infrastructure exists to support the project.
Guarantees	A legal promise made by a third party (guar-antor) to cover a borrower's debt or other types of liability in case of the borrower's default
Global Warming/ Climate Change	The process by which the earth is heating up due to an increase of greenhouse gases trapping heat from the sun, warming the earth.

Heat Rate	The amount of fuel required to generate a kilowatt-hour (kwh) of electricity.
Hedging arrangements	An instrument used to limit exposure to a price or unit of value that fluctuates. These typically cover interest rate, foreign currency exchange rates or commodity prices and/or inflation.
High Voltage Alternating Current (HVAC)	An electric power transmission system that uses alternating current for the bulk transmission of electrical power. Alternating current is the form in which electric power is generated by wind turbines and delivered to an end user.
High voltage direct current (HVDC)	An electric power transmission system that uses direct current for the bulk transmission of electrical power. For long-distance transmission, HVDC systems may offer lifetime cost advantages over HVAC systems. They are currently only used for point-to-point connections.
Hurdle Rate	A minimum acceptable internal rate of return (IRR). Projects generating returns in excess of the corporate hurdle rate are viable candidates for implementation.
Indemnity	A legal obligation to cover a liability.
Independent Engineer (IE)	A consulting firm that helps lenders by evaluating the technical aspects of a project (e.g., completion schedule, technical feasibility, and so on). Also, see definition for **Lenders' Engineer**.
Information Memorandum	A document that describes the project and the financing details; issued in connection with a loan syndication.
Infrastructure Project	A project in one of the following industrial sectors: power (electricity and gas), telecom, transportation, or water/sewage.

Internal Rate of Return (IRR)	The discount rate that makes the net present value equal to zero.
IFC Safeguards	All projects undergoing the International Finance Corporation's (IFC) initial credit review process after January 1, 2012 must follow: • The Policy on Environmental and Social Sustainability, which defines IFC's commitments to environmental and social sustainability; • The Performance Standards, which define clients' responsibilities for managing their environmental and social risks; and • The Access to Information Policy, which articulates IFC's commitment to transparency.
Investors	Parties who provide capital to the project enabling it to commence, seeking to make gains on the monies provided in the form of interest payments or a proportion of profits from the project (i.e., equity return).
Key Performance Indicators (KPIs)	Benchmarks to measure performance and of the project, or the parties' contribution to the project. These are typically referenced to the output specification and are the benchmark against which the developer is incentivised to perform. If the developer falls short of the performance indicators then typically deductions will be made and in persistent or material circumstances, a right of termination may arise.

Least Developed Countries (LDCs)	According to the United Nations, the Least Developed Countries represent the poorest and weakest segment of the international community. Around 12 percent of the world's population (880 million people) are estimated to live in these countries. LDCs are characterized by the following: • Weak human and institutional capacities • Low and unequally distributed income • Scarcity of domestic financial resources • Governance crisis, political instability and, in some cases, internal and external conflicts.
Lenders' Engineer	An engineering firm that advises lenders on technical matters. Also, see definition for **Independent Engineer**.
Letter of Intent (LOI)	A letter from one company to another acknowledging a willingness and ability to do business.
Levelized Cost of Energy (LCOE)	Levelized cost of energy is a commonly used measure of the cost of electricity production. It is defined as the revenue required (from whatever source) to earn a rate of return on investment equal to the WACC (see as follows) over the life of the energy-generating asset farm. Tax and inflation are not modeled.
Liquidated damages (LDs)	A specified monetary amount paid for a specific contractual breach that aims to compensate the injured party for the loss it suffers for such breach. Such amounts are agreed up front and in many common law jurisdictions must be a genuine pre-estimate of loss to withstand challenges that such regimes are unenforceable because they are deemed a penalty.

Low Carbon Energy	Any energy source that does not produce a high amount of carbon dioxide emissions, preferentially producing none at all.
Maintenance Reserve Account	A reserve account that builds up cash balances sufficient to cover a project's maintenance expenses.
Maturity	The final date a project finance loan is payable.
Merchant Power Plant (MPP)	A power plant that sells electricity without a long-term power purchase agreement.
Monte Carlo Simulation	The use of a random number generator to quantify the effects of uncertainty in a financial model.
Novation	The transfer of rights and obligations from one contracting party (which is released of those obligation) to a third party, with the agreement of each of the other contracting parties.
Offtake Agreements	An offtake agreement is an arrangement between a producer and a buyer to purchase or sell portions of the producer's upcoming goods. An offtake agreement is normally negotiated prior to the construction of an energy production facility—solar/wind farm and so on—to secure a market for its future output.
Operations and Maintenance (O&M) Agreement	A contract obligating a party to operate and maintain a project.
Operational Expenditure (OpEX)	Spend on all activities from works completion date until decommissioning.

| Operations, Maintenance and Service (OMS) | Can vary across different types of energy-generating assets. For offshore wind farms, OMS will cover both offshore and onshore transmission.

Definitions of O, M, and S are as follows:

Operation: Day-to-day management including all the work not covered under maintenance and service. For wind farm OMS, this includes cost for port facilities, buildings, management personnel, environmental monitoring, and community engagement.

Maintenance of assets: Scheduled (that is, planned a long time in advance) maintenance, which may be based on suppliers' recommendations or owner's experience. It includes condition-based or time-based maintenance programs and planned health and safety inspections. Typical maintenance includes inspection, checking of bolted joints, and replacement of wear parts (with design life less than the design life of the project).

Service of assets: Unscheduled interventions in response to events or failures. Interventions may be proactive (before failure occurs, for example responding to inspections or condition monitoring (CM) or reactive (after failure that affects generation has occurred). Also included are interventions due to major components not lasting the full turbine design life, even if intervention was planned prior to construction. Service operations include both on site repair and replacement of large and small components |

Pari Passu	Literal meaning, "with equal treatment among themselves." A legal term that refers to financial instruments that rank equally in right of payment with each other and with other instruments of the same issuer. Applies to both the right to be paid from available operating cash flow and the rights is the event of liquidation.
Partial Credit Guarantee (PCG)	An instrument designed to cover private lenders against all risks during a specified period of the financing term of debt for a public investment. These guarantees are designed to extend maturities and improve commercial terms.
Partial Risk Guarantee (PRG)	An instrument designed to cover private lenders against the risk that a government or government-owned agency fails to perform its contractual obligations vis-à-vis a private project.
Performance Bonds	Guarantees purchased by the project developer issued by commercial banks or insurance companies to guarantee full and successful implementation of a contract according to prespecified performance guidelines.
Performance specification	The document outlining the way in which the project must be operated throughout the life of the concession agreement and typically includes key performance indicators (KPIs).
Political Risk	Eight risks associate with cross-border investment and financing: *currency inconvertibility, expropriation, war and insurrection*, terrorism, environmental activities, landowner actions, nongovernmental activists, and legal and bureaucratic approvals. Those in bold are insurable. There is an overlap with the political element of *force majeure* risk.

Power Purchase Agreement (PPA)	A PPA is a long-term electricity supply agreement between two parties, usually between a power producer and a customer (an electricity consumer or trader). The PPA defines the conditions of the agreement, such as the amount of electricity to be supplied, negotiated prices, accounting, and penalties for noncompliance. A PPA is the principal agreement that defines the revenue and credit quality of a generating project and is thus a key instrument of project finance.
Project Company	A special-purpose entity created to develop, own, and operate a project.
Project Completion	Occurs when a defined set of technical and financial tests have been met as stipulated in the financing documents.
Project Finance	Involves a corporate sponsor investing in and owning a single-purpose industrial asset (usually with a limited life) through a legally independent entity financed with nonrecourse debt.
Request for Proposals (RFP)	An invitation to bid on a public procurement.
Senior debt	Money that is borrowed by the Developer to finance a project that takes priority over any "junior" debt (lower down the order of priority) or equity in the event that the Project Company becomes insolvent.
Shareholders Agreement	The generic term for any contract between two or more shareholders governing their conduct in relationship to the corporation, or partnership, in which they own shares.
Solar PV Panels	Solar photovoltaic panels convert light from the sun into electricity as a form of green energy.

Sovereign Guarantee	A government guarantee of its obligations under project documents.
Special Purpose Vehicle (SPV)	An entity established for a particular purpose, such as obtaining off-balance sheet financing or isolating the sponsors' other assets from the project's creditors.
Sponsor	A parent company or individual(s) that develops a project, for the purposes of this book, also known as the developer. Collectively used the term can include the major project parties such as construction contractor and commonly includes financial investors or funds.
Standby Letter of Credit	A letter of credit that provides for payment to a beneficiary when that beneficiary provides certification that certain obligations have been not been fulfilled.

Sustainable Development Goals (SDGs)	All United Nations Member States adopted the Sustainable Development Goals (SDGs), also known as the Global Goals, in 2015 as a universal call to action to end poverty, protect the planet, and ensure that all people enjoy peace and prosperity by 2030. At its heart are the 17 SDGs, which are an urgent call for action by all countries—developed and developing—in a global partnership. They recognize that ending poverty and other deprivations must go hand-in-hand with strategies that improve health and education, reduce inequality, and spur economic growth—all while tackling climate change and working to preserve our oceans and forests. Through the pledge to "Leave No One Behind," countries have committed to fast-track progress for those furthest behind first.
Sustainable Return on Investment (SROI)	SROI is a methodology for identifying and quantifying the entire triple bottom line—environmental, societal, and economic impacts of investment in projects and initiatives. It allows organizations to determine how their projects add value by assigning a monetary value to environmental or social benefits, and therefore incorporating non-cash and external benefits.
Take-or-Pay Contract	A contract that creates an unconditional obligation on the part of the buyer (offtaker) to pay for the good or service even if it is not produced or available from the seller.
Tenor	The number of years a loan is outstanding.

Term Sheet	A document that outlines in general terms the key agreements to be contained in a legal document; sometimes called a letter of understanding (LOU) or a memorandum of understanding (MOU).
Tolling Agreement	An agreement under which a Project Company imposes tolling charges on each project user as compensation for processing raw material.
Underwrite	An arrangement under which a financial house agrees to buy a certain agreed amount of securities of a new issue on a given date and at a given price, thereby assuring the issuer the full proceeds of the financing.
Vendor Finance	Debt provided by a supplier of equipment or services to the Project Company.
Warranty	A guarantee that a given fact will exist at some future date, as promised.
Witholding Tax	A tax on interest, royalty, or dividend payments, usually those paid overseas.
Weighted Average Cost of Capital (WACC)	The weighted average rate of return a developer expects to compensate itself and its internal and external investors over the life of a project.
Works Completion Date (WCD)	Date at which construction works are deemed complete and the wind farm, solar PV farm, or other energy-generating asset is handed to the operations team. In reality, this may take place over a period of time.

List of Organizations

African Development Bank (AfDB)	AfDB is a multilateral development finance institution. The AfDB was founded in 1964 and comprises three entities: The African Development Bank, the African Development Fund, and the Nigeria Trust Fund. The AfDB's mission is to fight poverty and improve living conditions on the continent through promoting the investment of public and private capital in projects and programs that are likely to contribute to the economic and social development of the region.
African Export Import Bank (Afrexim)	Also referred to as Afreximbank, is a pan-African multilateral trade finance institution created in 1993 under the umbrella of the African Development Bank. Afreximbank's mandate is to finance and promote intra- and extra-African trade using three broad services: credit (trade finance and project finance); risk bearing (guarantees and credit insurance); trade information and advisory services.
African Finance Corporation (AFC)	AFC is a multilateral financial institution, created by sovereign African states to provide pragmatic solutions to Africa's infrastructure deficit and challenging operating environment, by developing and financing infrastructure, natural resources, and industrial assets for the enhanced productivity and economic growth of African states. The AFC bridges the infrastructure investment gap through the provision of debt and equity finance, project development, technical and financial advisory services.

Asian Development Bank (ADB)	ADB is committed to achieving a prosperous, inclusive, resilient, and sustainable Asia and the Pacific, while sustaining its efforts to eradicate extreme poverty. Established in 1966, it is owned by 68 members—49 from the region. ADB assists its members, and partners, by providing loans, technical assistance, grants, and equity investments to promote social and economic development. ADB maximizes the development impact of its assistance by facilitating policy dialogues, providing advisory services, and mobilizing financial resources through financing operations that tap official, commercial, and export credit sources.
COP	Conference of the Parties (COP) is the supreme decision-making body of the UN Convention. All States that are Parties to the Convention are represented at the COP, at which they review the implementation of the Convention and any other legal instruments that the COP adopts and take decisions necessary to promote the effective implementation of the Convention, including institutional and administrative arrangements.
COP 26	The UK will host the 26th UN Climate Change Conference of the Parties (COP26) at the Scottish Event Campus (SEC) in Glasgow on 1–12 November 2021. The 26th session of the Conference of the Parties (COP 26) to the UNFCCC was originally set to take place from 9 to 19 November 2020, in Glasgow, Scotland, UK, but was postponed due to the COVID 19 pandemic.

Development Finance Institutions (DFI)	DFI also known as a development bank or development finance company (DFC) is a financial institution that provides risk capital for economic development projects on noncommercial basis.
European Bank for Reconstruction and Development (EBRD)	EBRD was founded in 1991 to create a new post–Cold War era in central and eastern Europe. EBRD is an international financial institution designed to foster transition toward open market-oriented economies and to promote private and entrepreneurial development across 30 countries in Central and Eastern Europe, Central Asia, and, since 2011, the Southern and Eastern Mediterranean region.
European Investment Bank (EIB)	EIB is a publicly owned international financial institution whose shareholders are the EU member states. It was established in 1958 under the Treaty of Rome as a policy-driven bank using financing operations to further EU policy goals. It is the world's largest international public lending institution.
Financial Times Stock Exchange Group (FTSE)	The Financial Times Stock Exchange Group (FTSE), also known by the nickname of "Footsie," is an independent organization. It is similar to the Standard & Poor's, which specializes in creating index offerings for the global financial markets.

Inter-American Development Bank	IADB was established in 1959 and supports Latin American and Caribbean economic development, social development, and regional integration by lending to governments and government agencies, including State corporations. IADB provide loans, grants, and technical assistance and conducts extensive research. The Bank's current focus areas include three development challenges—social inclusion and equality, productivity and innovation, and economic integration; three cross-cutting issues—gender equality and diversity, climate change and environmental sustainability as well as institutional capacity and the rule of law.
Islamic Development Bank (IDB)	IDB is a multilateral development bank, working to improve the lives by promoting social and economic development in 57 Member countries and Muslim communities worldwide, delivering impact at scale. IDB provide the infrastructure to enable people to lead better lives and achieve their full potential. They build collaborative partnerships between communities and nations, across our 57 member nations. IDB bring together the public and private sectors as well as with civil societies and the development sector through public–private partnerships and other joint projects.

International Finance Corporation (IFC)	The IFC was established in 1956 as a member of the World Bank Group, focused on investing in economic development. IFC provides financing of private-enterprise investment in developing countries around the world, through both loans and direct investments. Affiliated with the World Bank, it also provides advisory services to encourage the development of private enterprise in nations that might be lacking the necessary infrastructure or liquidity for businesses to secure financing.
International Monetary Fund (IMF)	IMF promotes international financial stability and monetary cooperation. It also facilitates international trade, promotes employment and sustainable economic growth, and helps to reduce global poverty. The IMF is governed by and accountable to its 189 member countries. Countries contribute funds to a pool through a quota system from which countries experiencing balance of payments problems can borrow money. Through the fund and other activities such as the gathering of statistics and analysis, surveillance of its members' economies, and the demand for particular policies, the IMF works to improve the economies of its member countries.
Morgan Stanley Capital International (MSCI)	MSCI is an acronym for Morgan Stanley Capital International. An investment research firm provides stock indexes, portfolio risk and performance analytics, and governance tools to institutional investors and hedge funds.

Multilateral Investment Guarantee Agency (MIGA)	MIGA is an international institution that promotes investment in developing countries by offering political and economic risk insurance. By promoting foreign direct investment into developing countries, the agency aims to support economic growth, reduce poverty, and improve people's lives. MIGA is a member of the World Bank Group and has 181 member states (156 developing nations and another 25 industrialized countries) as of March 2020.
Multilateral Lending Agencies	Organizations jointly owned by a group of countries and designed to promote international and regional economic cooperation. These lending agencies may have such goals as aiding development and furthering social and economic growth in member countries. Also known as "multilateral agencies."
Net Zero Asset Owner Alliance	United Nations-Convened Net-Zero Asset Owner Alliance is an international group of institutional investors delivering on a bold commitment to transition their investment portfolios to net-zero GHG emissions by 2050. Convened by UN Environment Program's Finance Initiative (UNEP FI) and the Principles for Responsible Investment (PRI), the Alliance is supported by WWF and is part of the Mission 2020 campaign, an initiative led by Christiana Figueres, former Executive Secretary of the United Nations Framework Convention on Climate Change (UNFCCC).

Nordic Investment Bank (NIB)	The Nordic Investment Bank is the international financial institution of the Nordic and Baltic countries. NIB acquires the funds for its lending by borrowing on the international capital markets. NIB mission is to finance projects that improve the productivity and benefit the environment of the Nordic and Baltic countries. NIB provides sustainable, long-term financing to customers in both the private and public sectors on competitive market terms to complement commercial lending.
Standard & Poor's (S&P)	Standard & Poor's (S&P) is a leading index provider and data source of independent credit ratings. It is also the provider of the popular S&P 500 Index. S&P was founded in 1860, offering financial market intelligence.
United Nations (UN)	The United Nations is an international organization founded in 1945. It is currently made up of 193 Member States. The mission and work of the UN is guided by the purposes and principles contained in its founding charter. UN aims to sustain international peace and security, develop friendly relations among nations, attain international cooperation, and be a center for harmonizing the actions of nations. It is the largest, most familiar, most internationally represented and most powerful intergovernmental organization in the world.

United Nations Development Program (UNDP)	UNDP is the United Nations' global development network and is funded entirely by voluntary contributions from UN member states. The organization operates in 177 countries where it works with local governments to meet development challenges and develop local capacity. It works internationally to help countries achieve SDGs. The UNDP provides expert advice, training, and grants support to developing countries, with increasing emphasis on assistance to the least developed countries.
World Bank	World Bank is an international financial institution that provides loans and grants to the governments of poorer countries for the purpose of pursuing capital projects. It comprises two institutions: the International Bank for Reconstruction and Development (IBRD) and the International Development Association (IDA). The World Bank is a component of the World Bank Group. Its aim is to end extreme poverty.
World Bank Group	Five institutions under one group. Consists of IBRD (The International Bank for Reconstruction and Development); IDA (The International Development Association); IFC (The International Finance Corporation); MIGA (The Multilateral Investment Guarantee Agency); ICSID (The International Centre for Settlement of Investment Disputes)

References

Esty, B.C. 2004. *Modern Project Finance: A Casebook.* Hoboken, NJ: John Wiley & Sons, Inc.

Global Infrastructure Hub. 2016. *Allocating Risks in Public-Private Partnership Contracts.* Sydney: GI Hub.
https://aiche.org/ifs/total-cost-assessment-methodology
https://earthshiftglobal.com/consultingservices/start-sustainability-return-on-investment-roi-engagement

Leiva, B. 2019. "Energy's Place in Economic Theory." https://researchgate.net/publication/332739333

REN21. 2020. *Renewables 2020 Global Status Report.* Paris: REN21 Secretariat.

Yescombe, E.R. 2014. *Principles of Project Finance.* Oxford: Academic Press.

Zencey, E. 2014. "Energy as Master Resource." https://researchgate.net/publication/287831825

About the Author

Francis Ugboma heads the energy team of a large municipality in London. In this role, he oversees energy and carbon-related strategy, the development of infrastructure projects, and the operations around low-carbon smart district energy systems. His energy services team is one of the most innovative in the UK and a pioneer in municipal sustainability. In 2021, the team brought into operation the world's first mass transit waste heat district heating project which takes waste heat from the London Underground transport system and uses it to provide low-carbon heating to over 1,500 homes.

Ugboma's career has been focused on developing and financing energy projects for some of the world's leading energy players including ENI, Lukoil, and EDF. As a project developer, he worked on the first integrated liquefied natural gas (LNG) to power project in the world from tender to financial close and was instrumental in the structuring of the key financing agreements of the €400 million project. He later secured a 20-year concession agreement for a similar project in West Africa.

Ugboma earned a bachelor's degree in Civil and Environmental Engineering from University College London and a master's in Business Administration from the IESE Business School in Barcelona. He speaks five languages including French, Spanish, and Italian. He is also an Affiliate Member of the Energy Institute and a Chartered Engineer (Stage 1).

Drawing from over twenty years of hands-on experience in the sustainable energy sector, this practical guide will be a valuable resource to both those considering and those who are already involved in projects in both developing and developed countries.

Index

OTHER TITLES IN THE ECONOMICS AND PUBLIC POLICY COLLECTION

Jeffrey Edwards, North Carolina A&T State University, Editor

- *Understanding Economic Equilibrium* by Mike Shaw, Thomas J. Cunningham, and Rosemary Cunningham
- *Macroeconomics, Third Edition* by David G. Tuerck
- *Negotiation Booster* by Kasia Jagodzinska
- *Mastering the Moneyed Mind, Volume IV* by Christopher Bayer
- *Mastering the Moneyed Mind, Volume III* by Christopher Bayer
- *Mastering the Moneyed Mind, Volume II* by Christopher Bayer
- *Mastering the Moneyed Mind, Volume I* by Christopher Bayer
- *Understanding the Indian Economy from the Post-Reforms of 1991, Volume II* by Shrawan Kumar Singh
- *Understanding the Indian Economy from the Post-Reforms of 1991, Volume I* by Shrawan Kumar Singh
- *Business Liability and Economic Damages, Second Edition* by Scott D. Gilbert
- *The Economics of Online Gaming* by Andrew Wagner
- *Global Sustainable Capitalism* by Marcus Goncalves, Mario Svigir, and Harry Xia
- *Political Dimensions of the American Macroeconomy* by Gerald T. Fox

Concise and Applied Business Books

The Collection listed above is one of 30 business subject collections that Business Expert Press has grown to make BEP a premiere publisher of print and digital books. Our concise and applied books are for...

- Professionals and Practitioners
- Faculty who adopt our books for courses
- Librarians who know that BEP's Digital Libraries are a unique way to offer students ebooks to download, not restricted with any digital rights management
- Executive Training Course Leaders
- Business Seminar Organizers

Business Expert Press books are for anyone who needs to dig deeper on business ideas, goals, and solutions to everyday problems. Whether one print book, one ebook, or buying a digital library of 110 ebooks, we remain the affordable and smart way to be business smart. For more information, please visit www.businessexpertpress.com, or contact sales@businessexpertpress.com.

www.ingramcontent.com/pod-product-compliance
Lightning Source LLC
Chambersburg PA
CBHW061320220326
41599CB00026B/4964